Shining
with joy
PHILIPPIANS
by Steven J. Lawson

thegoodbook
COMPANY

Philippians For You

If you are reading *Philippians For You* alongside this Good Book Guide, here is how the studies in this booklet link to the chapters of *Philippians For You*:

Study One → Ch 1-2
Study Two → Ch 3-5
Study Three → Ch 6, 8
Study Four → Ch 7

Study Five → Ch 9-11
Study Six → Ch 12-13
Study Seven → Ch 14-15

Find out more about *Philippians For You* at:
www.thegoodbook.com/for-you

Shining with joy
The Good Book Guide to Philippians
© Steven J. Lawson/The Good Book Company, 2017. Reprinted 2017, 2018 (twice).
Series Consultants: Tim Chester, Tim Thornborough,
                    Anne Woodcock, Carl Laferton

The Good Book Company
Tel: (US): 866 244 2165
Tel (UK): 0333 123 0880
Email (US): info@thegoodbook.com
Email (UK): info@thegoodbook.co.uk

Websites
North America: www.thegoodbook.com
UK: www.thegoodbook.co.uk
Australia: www.thegoodbook.com.au
New Zealand: www.thegoodbook.co.nz

Unless otherwise indicated, Scripture quotations taken from the New American Standard Bible® (NASB), Copyright © 1960, 1962, 1963, 1968, 1971, 1972, 1973, 1975, 1977, 1995 by The Lockman Foundation. Used by permission. www.Lockman.org

ISBN: 9781784981181

Printed in Turkey

CONTENTS

Introduction: Good Book Guides

Every Bible-study group is different—yours may take place in a church building, in a home or in a cafe, on a train, over a leisurely mid-morning coffee or squashed into a 30-minute lunch break. Your group may include new Christians, mature Christians, non-Christians, moms and tots, students, businessmen or teens. That's why we've designed these *Good Book Guides* to be flexible for use in many different situations.

Our aim in each session is to uncover the meaning of a passage, and see how it fits into the "big picture" of the Bible. But that can never be the end. We also need to appropriately apply what we have discovered to our lives. Let's take a look at what is included:

⊕ **Talkabout:** Most groups need to "break the ice" at the beginning of a session, and here's the question that will do that. It's designed to get people talking around a subject that will be covered in the course of the Bible study.

⊕ **Investigate:** The Bible text for each session is broken up into manageable chunks, with questions that aim to help you understand what the passage is about. The **Leader's Guide** contains **guidance for questions**, and sometimes ⊗ additional "follow-up" questions.

⊕ **Explore more (optional):** These questions will help you connect what you have learned to other parts of the Bible, so you can begin to fit it all together like a jig-saw; or occasionally look at a part of the passage that's not dealt with in detail in the main study.

⊖ **Apply:** As you go through a Bible study, you'll keep coming across **apply** sections. These are questions to get the group discussing what the Bible teaching means in practice for you and your church. ⊡ **Getting personal** is an opportunity for you to think, plan and pray about the changes that you personally may need to make as a result of what you have learned.

⊕ **Pray:** We want to encourage prayer that is rooted in God's word—in line with his concerns, purposes and promises. So each session ends with an opportunity to review the truths and challenges highlighted by the Bible study, and turn them into prayers of request and thanksgiving.

The **Leader's Guide** and introduction provide historical background information, explanations of the Bible texts for each session, ideas for **optional extra** activities, and guidance on how best to help people uncover the truths of God's word.

Why study Philippians?

"Rejoice in the Lord always; again I will say, rejoice!" (Philippians 4 v 4)

God never commands us to do what he does not enable us to do. And through Paul's letter to the church in Philippi, in modern-day northeastern Greece, God both tells us to rejoice and also gives us great reason to rejoice—whatever we are facing in life.

Joy is a spiritual grace that we all need to experience in our Christian lives. We live in a world of stress and anxiety that all too easily and subtly can steal the peace of God from our hearts. We need an abundant, overflowing joy to flood our souls. The book of Philippians is written for that very purpose—to point us to that joy.

It does so by focusing us on the gospel. There is a repeated emphasis upon the good news of salvation that is in God's Son, Jesus Christ (1 v 5, 7, 12, 16, 27; 2 v 22; 4 v 3, 15). Paul places great stress upon the saving message of the gospel, as well as the need for us to live it out in our daily lives. The believers needed a gospel focus. We are no different.

But Philippians also produces joy in us by showing us how to grow in holiness. This letter teaches us much about how to live the Christian life. Paul will tell us that we bear great responsibility to work out our salvation in fear and trembling (2 v 12-13). At the same time, he will instruct us that it is God who is at work within us for his good pleasure. Expect to grow in a desire for holiness and a life of holiness as you walk through this letter.

It is wonderful to know that the great truths of Philippians apply to us, if we are in Christ Jesus. In these seven studies, you can look forward to learning more and experiencing more of the fullness of what God has prepared for us as his people, so that you may enjoy shining "as lights in the world, holding fast the word of life" (2 v 15-16).

Note: This Good Book Guide is based on the New American Standard Bible translation, but it has been written in such a way that it works equally well with the English Standard Version and New International Version.

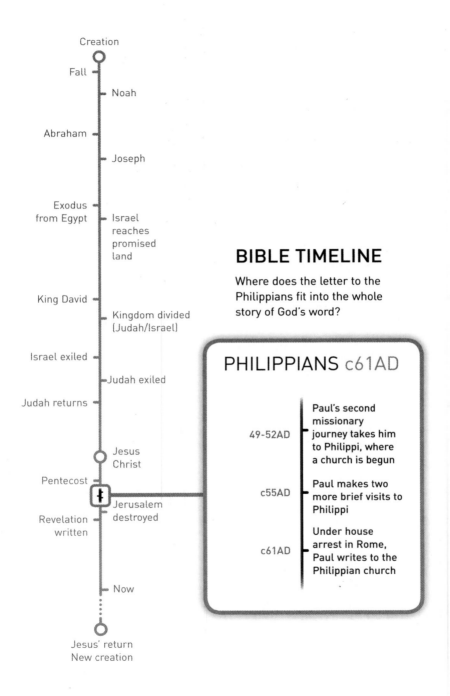

Creation
Fall
Noah
Abraham
Joseph
Exodus from Egypt
Israel reaches promised land
King David
Kingdom divided (Judah/Israel)
Israel exiled
Judah exiled
Judah returns
Jesus Christ
Pentecost
Jerusalem destroyed
Revelation written
Now
Jesus' return New creation

BIBLE TIMELINE

Where does the letter to the Philippians fit into the whole story of God's word?

PHILIPPIANS c61AD

49-52AD	Paul's second missionary journey takes him to Philippi, where a church is begun
c55AD	Paul makes two more brief visits to Philippi
c61AD	Under house arrest in Rome, Paul writes to the Philippian church

1 Philippians 1 v 1-11
JOY-FILLED PRAYER

⊕ talkabout

1. What do you think you can tell about someone from whether they pray, who they pray to, and what they pray?

⊕ investigate

▶ Read Philippians 1 v 1-8

2. What is notable about the way the writers of this letter—the apostle Paul and his co-worker Timothy—describe themselves (v 1)?

• How do they describe the recipients?

⊡ explore more

▶ Read Acts 16 v 6-40

Why did Paul go to Philippi (v 6-10)?

Whom did God call to saving faith through Paul (v 11-34)?

What do you think this taught Paul, and this new church, about:
- *who God can save?*
- *what circumstances God can work in?*

3. What is Paul doing, and how is he feeling (v 3-4)?

- Where is Paul as he writes (v 7, see also v 13-14)?

- How does this make his prayer and his emotion in verses 3-4 all the more striking?

☺ getting personal

In the midst of our own adversities, we should never lose sight of praying for others. When offering intercessory prayers, we are diverted away from our own problems to the lives of others. This kind of selfless praying is good medicine for our own troubled souls because it takes our gaze off of ourselves and refocuses it upon others.

Have you experienced this in your own life?

How might you reshape your prayers in light of this?

4. What is the cause of Paul's joyful thanksgiving (v 5, 7)?

5. Why is Paul sure his Christian friends will keep going in their faith (v 6)?

- Why is this confidence necessary for enabling him to pray with joyful thanks?

6. What impression of Paul do these verses give you?

⤷ apply

7. Given who Christ is and what he offers (v 2), why is it a privilege, rather than oppressive, to be one of his "bond-servants"?

⬇ investigate

8. What does Paul's prayer teach us about what love in action looks like?

☺ getting personal

No matter how doctrinally sound we may be, if we are without love, we are "as sounding brass, or a tinkling cymbal" (1 Corinthians 13 v 1). Without love for others, regardless of how involved we are in Christian activities, we are "nothing."

Does this encourage you, or challenge you, or both?

9. What does Paul's prayer teach us about what the purpose of the Christian life is (v 11)?

The word "sincere" or "pure" (NIV/ESV) in verse 10 comes from two words for "sun" and "to judge." In ancient times, devious merchants would conceal flaws in their expensive pottery with wax. The authenticity of valuable pottery was revealed when held up to the light of the sun—it was "sincere."

10. So what is Paul teaching in verse 10 about what our aim must be as Christians?

⇥ apply

11. How do the priorities of Paul's prayer here compare with our prayers?

* If or where yours are different, what might this suggest about your view of God, or what matters to you in life?

12. In what areas is your sincerity tested? What would an authentically loving Christian life look like when those tests come?

⇧ pray

Use verses 3-6 to thank God for each other, and for the members of your church.

Then use verses 9-11 to pray for one another and for your church. Share any personal circumstances you would like to pray about, discussing together how these verses might shape your prayers for each other.

2 Philippians 1 v 12-30
JOY IN HARDSHIPS

The story so far

Paul is writing to the church in Philippi, thanking God joyfully and confidently for their faith and praying that they would abound in love, to God's glory.

⊕ talkabout

1. What makes you feel joyful?

   • What types of circumstances, or what actions of other people, can make you feel less good?

⊕ investigate

▶ Read Philippians 1 v 12-20

2. What reasons does Paul have for not feeling good about life (v 12-17)?

3.   How is he responding (v 18)?

- Why?
- v 12-13

- v 14

- v 18

In one sense, Paul is facing a very uncertain and difficult future.

4.   But what is he confident of (v 19-20)?

⊡ **explore more**

What are the gospel preachers Paul mentions in verses 15-17 motivated by?

❯ **Read 1 Thessalonians 2 v 3-9**

What was Paul's gospel proclamation motivated by?

❯ **Read 1 Peter 5 v 1-4**

What wrong motives could drive church leaders?

What right motives should drive church leaders?

What would bad motivations and godly motivations look like in your own life, in terms of your gospel proclamation and your serving within your church?

➔ apply

5. What prevents us from responding to difficult times as Paul did?

- Think of a trial you have recently faced (or are facing now). What would it look like to respond in the same way as Paul?

☺ getting personal

Do you care more about your reputation or your Redeemer's? About your comfort or about Christ being made known?

You are not where you are—in good times and in bad—by accident. You are where you are by divine appointment, for the purposes of sharing the gospel.

In which part of your life does this need to transform your perspective and your priorities? How?

⬇ investigate

▶ Read Philippians 1 v 21-26

6. What reason does verse 21 reveal for Paul's attitude in verses 12-20?

> **DICTIONARY**
>
> **Flesh (v 22, 24):** here, Paul means his mortal body.

7.   What is Paul's dilemma (v 22-26)?

• What does he conclude is the best outcome, and why?

⊡ **getting personal**

It is only when you know that death will usher you into the presence of God that you will live with fearless faith. No one is ready to live until they are ready to die.

Can you say of your own outlook on life, "To live is Christ and to die is gain"? Why / why not? If not, what would it take for your answer to change?

❯ **Read Philippians 1 v 27-30**

8.   How does tell Paul his readers to conduct their lives (v 27)?

DICTIONARY

Conduct (v 27): behave.

9.   What words does Paul use in these verses to describe the faithful Christian life (v 27b-29)?

➔ apply

10. The gospel is good news, but it is not easy news. How has Paul shown us this in verses 21-30?

11. What goes wrong when we forget that...
- the gospel is good news?

- the gospel is not easy news?

12. What have these verses shown us about how to live a joyful life?

⬆ pray

Spend time praising God together, and thanking him that "to die is gain." Then share ways that you are struggling to live for Christ, and hold loose to your comfort and reputation—and pray for a joyful, uncompromising approach to obeying him.

3 Philippians 2 v 1-11, 19-30
JOY AND HUMILITY

The story so far

Paul is writing to the church in Philippi, thanking God joyfully and confidently for their faith and praying that they would abound in love, to God's glory.

For the believer, to live is Christ and to die is gain—so the Philippians (and we) can live with joy, even in difficult circumstances, standing firm in faith together.

⊕ talkabout

1. What is humility?

- In what circumstances does your society celebrate humility? In what ways does it see humility as negative?

⊕ investigate

Humility is the central theme that runs throughout Philippians 2. The actual word "humility" is found in verse 3, but the concept is seen throughout this entire section.

> **Read Philippians 2 v 1-4**

Each "if" in verse 1 can equally accurately be translated "since" or "because."

2. What do the Philippian Christians enjoy (v 1)?

3. If/since this is true of them, what does Paul appeal for (v 2-4)?

4. How do verses 2-4 define what it means to have "humility" of mind?

▶ Read Philippians 2 v 5-11

5. Why is Jesus the supreme example of humility (v 6-8)?

DICTIONARY
Bestowed on (v 9): gave.

• How does this make verse 5 a great challenge to us?

6. How did God the Father respond to the humility of God the Son (v 9-11)?

• How does this encourage us to live with "humility" of mind?

⊡ explore more

> **❯ Read Luke 18 v 9-14**

How does Jesus teach here what Paul does in Philippians 2 about pride, humility, and exaltation?

What does this teach us about the link between our humility and our prayers?

⊖ apply

7. Think of some specific ways in which living with this kind of attitude would mean blessing for those around you in…

• your church?

• your home?

• your workplace?

🙂 getting personal

Given this example of Jesus, it is clear that none of us can ever humble ourselves too much. None of us may ever say, "Enough. I deserve better, so I will stop here."

How does this challenge you? When do you find it hardest to live with Christ-like humility?

True humility will never be forgotten by God. He will see it, note it, and reward it. No one ever truly humbles themselves before God without being exalted by God, in this life or in the life to come.

How does this encourage you? How will it change how you live in those times when it is hard to be humble?

⤓ investigate

▶ Read Philippians 2 v 19-30

8.   How does Timothy show us what humility looks like in real life (v 19-23)?

DICTIONARY

Kindred (v 20): family-like.
Furtherance (v 22): advance.
Minister (v 25): here, meaning one who attends to, or looks out for.
Deficient (v 30): lacking.

9.   Likewise, how does Epaphroditus show us what humility looks like in real life (v 26-30)?

10. How should the Philippian Christians think of and treat Epaphroditus (v 29)?

with honor / high regard

⊡ apply

11. Who is held "in high regard" (or "honored," NIV/ESV) in your church, and why? Would Timothy and Epaphroditus be? Why / why not?

12. Do you find their examples more or less challenging than the example of the Lord Jesus? Why?

⊡ getting personal

What would it look like for your life humbly to be given to God in a manner worthy of Paul's commendations of Epaphroditus? Be specific.

⊡ pray

Use verses 6-11 to praise the Lord Jesus Christ. Work through each verse, thanking him for who he is, what he has done, and where he is now.

Share an aspect of Timothy or Epaphroditus' humility that you would like God to grow in your own life, and use your answers as the basis of your prayers for one another.

4 Philippians 2 v 12-18

_8|26_

JOY IN OBEDIENCE

The story so far

Paul is writing to the church in Philippi, thanking God joyfully and confidently for their faith and praying that they would abound in love, to God's glory.

For the believer, to live is Christ and to die is gain—so the Philippians (and we) can live with joy, even in difficult circumstances, standing firm in faith together.

Humility, as exemplified by Jesus in his incarnation and crucifixion, is a central tenet of the Christian life, to be pursued and highly regarded by all of us.

⊕ talkabout

1. What should a Christian aim to do in the time between being saved and going to heaven?

⊕ investigate

▶ **Read Philippians 2 v 12-18**

This is addressed to Paul's "beloved" or "dear friends"—that is, Christians. If we miss this, it will lead us to falsely see these verses as teaching that someone must work to earn their salvation.

2. With that in mind, what do you understand Paul to be saying in verse 12?

DICTIONARY

Fear (v 12): healthy, reverential awe.
Disputing (v 14): arguing.
Perverse (v 15): distorted.
Lights (v 15): stars.
Drink offering (v 17): this was poured on top of an animal sacrifice to God. Paul's life is being poured out for the sake of the Philippians' faith.

3. Who is at work in the process of "sanctification"—that is, growing in holiness (v 12-13)?

4. In what way does verse 13 explain why Christians obey "with fear and trembling"? What should our view of God be?

⊖ apply

5. What goes wrong in our Christian lives if we…

• forget that we are called to work out our salvation, rather than work for our salvation?

• forget that God is at work?

• forget that we must be at work?

6. Why does a right view of God produce both joy and trembling?

• How can we encourage each other to have this view?

⊡ getting personal

Spiritual couch potatoes grow little in grace or holiness. Being in prayer, studying the Bible, and then obeying it in your life requires serious work.

How have you been motivated to enjoy growing in sanctification? In which areas in particular will you pray for God to work in you as you work at growing in godliness?

⊡ investigate

In verses 14-18, Paul gives us some specific application for daily living.

7. Why is verse 14 challenging?

• How does verse 15 motivate us to obey verse 14?

"Holding fast" (or "hold[ing] firmly" (v 16) more correctly carries the idea of "holding forth" or "holding out."

8. What is the link between obeying verse 14 and being able to "appear as lights [or stars, NIV] in the world, holding fast the word of life" (v 15-16)?

9. How will Paul feel as he sees the Philippians working out their salvation and holding out the word of life (v 17)?

• How should the Philippians feel about it (v 18)?

⊞ explore more

▶ **Read 1 Thessalonians 2 v 19 – 3 v 10**

How does this passage give us further insight into:
• *how Paul feels about his Christian friends?*
• *what Paul's priorities are for his Christian friends?*
• *what Paul told young churches they could expect their Christian lives to involve?*

⊡ getting personal

You can be, and should be, a channel for joy to flow through your life to other believers.

Do you share joy in the Lord with others, particularly when they are living through trying circumstances? Do you allow others to share Christian joy with you, particularly when you are in those trials?

➔ apply

10. When do you find it easiest to grumble? How could you turn those moments into opportunities to praise God and hold out the word of life?

11. What have we learned is necessary for effective witness?

• How have you seen this kind of effective witness, either in your own life or in those around you?

12. What have these verses shown you about how to shine with joy?

⬆ pray

Praise God for his work in you and purposes for you. Pray with humble thanks for ways you have seen him working in your lives.

Ask God to be at work in you, and to help you work as he works. Speak to him about particular ways you struggle to obey him, or ways you struggle to obey without grumbling.

Thank God that you are able to shine as a light in a dark world. Pray for particular people with whom you would love to share his gospel.

5 Philippians 3 v 1-21
JOY AS WE RUN

The story so far

For the believer, to live is Christ and to die is gain—so the Philippians (and we) can live with joy, even in difficult circumstances, standing firm in faith together.

Humility, as exemplified by Jesus in his incarnation and crucifixion, is a central tenet of the Christian life, to be pursued and highly regarded by all of us.

Christians must work out their salvation by obeying God more and more, so that they may shine as lights in this world, joyfully holding out the gospel.

⊕ talkabout

1. Imagine you had to spend a year outside of your own country. What do you think you would most miss about it? What would you most look forward to as you thought about returning?

⊕ investigate

▶ Read Philippians 3 v 1-11

2. What is the command in verse 1? What difference does it make that it is a command, not a request or encouragement?

3. What do you think Paul means when he talks about putting "confidence in the flesh" (v 3-4)? In what way are the "dogs" (false teachers) doing this (v 2)?

• How would such a view of life pollute Christian joy?

4. What did Paul place his confidence in:
• before his conversion (v 4-6)?

• after he turned to Christ as his Lord (v 7-11)?

⊡ **explore more**

"But..." Paul writes in verse 7. That one word points back to the day when Paul came to know Jesus Christ in a personal, saving way.

⊳ Read Acts 9 v 1-18

Why was Saul/Paul traveling to Damascus (v 1-2)?

What happened to change his plans, and his life?

How does Jesus characterize what Saul/Paul was seeking to do to the church (v 4)?

What does this episode, unique though it is, reveal generally about Christian conversion?

⊡ getting personal

Paul gives us his conversion in Philippians 3 in two stages: BC (Before Conversion) and AD (After Deliverance). He wants everyone to see how his life was revolutionized by Jesus Christ.

If you were in an elevator and had the opportunity to explain your own conversion, but had only a minute until you got out, how would you explain your own BC and AD in a way that gives glory to Christ's seeking of you, and not your decision to seek for him?

⊡ apply

5. In what kinds of ways do we see the same Christ-plus false teaching in our day that Paul saw in Philippi?

• Is Paul right to call such teachers "dogs"? Why / why not?

6. Imagine someone in your church has just been bullied in their workplace or has lost their job because of their loyalty to Christ. How do these verses teach you to encourage them?

⊕ investigate

> **Read Philippians 3 v 12-21**

7. How does Paul now view his past, his present, and his future (v 12-14)?

DICTIONARY

Perfect (v 15): or mature.
Subject (v 21): bring under authority.

• How do verses 20-21 excite believers about "what lies ahead"?

8. How does Paul want his readers to respond to his words?

• v 15

• v 16

• v 17

⊡ getting personal

Maturity occurs through imitating mature believers. Every Christian needs to have the same kinds of examples before them. Wise is the believer who has several such people in their life. Misguided is the believer who thinks they have no need of these types of influences.

Who is your mentor? Do you need humbly to ask an older Christian to serve you in this way?

Is there someone whom you could, in your turn, seek to mentor?

9. What are the alternative future and present that the "dogs" would lead this church into (v 19)?

⊖ apply

10. What are the appetites that your culture seeks to satisfy that lead to shame and destruction? Of those, which do you think are most likely to seep into the way Christ's people live within your culture?

11. How can you help one another to run hard for home?

12. What truths have given you cause for joy during this study? How will you remember them, and remind others of them?

⬆ pray

Use your answers to Question Twelve to prompt you to praise God joyfully.

Use your answers to Questions Ten and Eleven to shape your prayers for each other and for your church.

6 Philippians 4 v 1-9
JOY WHEN FACED WITH CONFLICT AND ANXIETY

The story so far

Humility, as exemplified by Jesus in his incarnation and crucifixion, is a central tenet of the Christian life, to be pursued and highly regarded by all of us.

Christians must work out their salvation by obeying God more and more, so that they may shine as lights in this world, joyfully holding out the gospel.

Authentic joy comes from having a personal relationship with God through Jesus as we walk toward our home with him. False teaching robs us of that joy.

⊕ talkabout

1. For what kinds of reasons do Christians who are in the same church fall out with one another? Does it matter?

• For what kinds of reasons do Christians worry? Does it matter?

⊕ investigate

▶ **Read Philippians 4 v 1-5**

2. What appears to be the problem that Paul is addressing?

3. What are we told about Euodia and Syntyche in verse 3? How does this underline the seriousness of what is happening within this church?

4. What commands and truths does Paul give in this situation, and who to? For each, consider how this command and/or truth would help the reconciliation of these women and resolve the conflict.

- v 1

- v 2

- v 3a

- v 3b

- v 4

- v 5a

- v 5b

➡ apply

5. Imagine Euodia and Syntyche are in your church. What has this passage taught you about how you need to respond?

* Imagine you are Euodia or Syntyche. What has this passage taught you about how you need to respond? How has it motivated you to obey?

⊡ getting personal

Rejoicing in all the Lord is to us and for us will tend to correct our perspective on everything else, especially in conflict. Those who will spend an eternity in joyful unity ought to start living in it now.

Is there any fellow Christian with whom you need to take steps to make peace? How will you do so?

Are there any fellow Christians whom you need to seek to bring together and encourage to make peace? How will you do that?

⊡ investigate

▶ **Read Philippians 4 v 6-9**

6. What is the cure for anxiety, according to verses 6-7?

> **DICTIONARY**
>
> **Supplication (v 6):** asking for things which we are lacking.
> **Good repute (v 8):** spoken well of.
> **Practice (v 9):** as in do.

7. What difference does it make that the beginning of verse 6 is a command, and not an aspiration?

- God never commands what he does not enable. What truths in verses 5-7 enable us to obey this command?

⊡ **explore more**

❯ **Read Matthew 6 v 25-34**

What does Jesus command his followers not to do, and to do?
- *v 25*   • *v 31*   • *v 33*   • *v 34*

What truths does he remind us of, to enable us to obey his commands?
- *v 25*   • *v 26, 30*   • *v 27*   • *v 32*   • *v 33*

⊡ **getting personal**

What are the three main sources of your anxiety today? How does that anxiety manifest itself in your emotions and your life?

Have you accepted that worry is the failure to believe the promises of God in his word?

How will you apply the cure for worry that Paul lays out in these verses?

8. How can we actively "dwell on" or "think about" Paul's list in verse 8?

9. What do you think would be the opposite of obeying verse 8?

⊖ apply

There is an inseparable connection between what we think about and how we live.

10. How have you experienced this, both positively and negatively, in your life?

11. What has this passage taught us are three great dangers to joy and peace?

• How can you encourage one another to avoid these pitfalls and so enjoy "the peace of God" (v 7)?

⬆ pray

Speak to God about any conflicts between Christians that you know of, especially if they are members of your church.

Share your greatest anxieties with your group, and then pray for one another with thanksgiving and petition. Ask God for a greater experience of his incomprehensible peace.

7 Philippians 4 v 10-23
JOY IN ALL THINGS

The story so far

Christians must work out their salvation by obeying God more and more, so that they may shine as lights in this world, joyfully holding out the gospel.

Authentic joy comes from having a personal relationship with God through Jesus as we walk toward our home with him. False teaching robs us of that joy.

Conflict in a church must be met with joy and overcome by remembering our unity. Anxiety within hearts needs to be met with joy and overcome by prayer.

⊕ talkabout

1. If there were one thing you could change or add to your life to make you more content, what would it be?

- What role do circumstances and wealth have to play in making us feel content in life?

⊕ investigate

▶ Read Philippians 4 v 10-13

As we consider Paul's words in these verses, as so often with this letter, we need to remember that his circumstances are anything but good. The apostle is imprisoned in Rome, chained to the elite Roman guards who serve in Caesar's household. He is awaiting

DICTIONARY

Want (v 11): need.
Humble means (v 12): a lack of everything.

trial before Caesar with his own life at stake, confined under house arrest, and unable to move about with freedom. The local pastors in Rome have become so envious of Paul's giftedness that they have resorted to a smear campaign against him. Epaphroditus, sent from the church in Philippi to assist Paul, has been sick almost to the point of death. Whatever could go wrong appears to have gone wrong.

2. What is Paul joyful about (v 10—verse 18 gives more detail on what Paul is referring to here)?

3. Was his joy and contentment dependent on this assistance (v 11)?

• Why / why not?

4. When is Paul content (v 11-12)?

5. Why is Paul content (v 13)?

• What do you think "all things" (or "all this," NIV) means (and does not mean) in this context?

⊖ apply

6. What is the secret of contentment? Where else do we look, or point other Christians to, to find it? Why?

7. Is it harder to find contentment in Christ when times are hard, or when times are good?

• How does verse 13 teach us to speak to one another about contentment when:
• things are going well?

• things are very hard?

⊡ getting personal

God had only one Son without sin, but he has no sons without sorrow. You will know what it is to be hungry. You may know what it is to be full. But this is the secret which Paul has let us know: you have all you can ever need in Christ, and you can do all things you need to through Christ, who strengthens you.

How does this speak to you today? Is it a comfort, or a challenge, or both?

⊡ investigate

❯ Read Philippians 4 v 14-23

8. How do these verses reveal the partnership between Paul and the Philippian church?

9. How does Paul describe the Philippians' financial giving in verse 18?

• What does he promise the Philippians about their finances in verse 19? Why is it important that he says "needs" and not "wants" or "wishes"?

⊡ explore more

▶ **Read 2 Corinthians 8 v 1-5, 9-15; 9 v 6-11**

Why did the Macedonian church give in the way they did (8 v 1-5, 9)?

What instructions for giving does Paul give in 8 v 10-15?

What do his readers need to believe (9 v 6-11)?

How does Paul's teaching here fit with, and add to, his words to the Philippians about their giving?

10. How are verses 20 and 23 fitting "Amens" with which to end this letter?

⊟ apply

11. Paul says there is great joy in giving generously and sacrificially. How does this compare with the view of the society in which you live?

• Which view do you tend to follow? How can you encourage each other as a church to listen to God's word in this area?

⊡ getting personal

When you realize that your financial support of God's servants is a fragrant sacrifice that brings great pleasure to God, as well as meeting the needs of God's ministers, you will find you are a sacrificial giver who can be classified as a "cheerful giver" (2 Corinthians 9 v 7).

Are you being prompted to change what you give, or the motivation for giving it? What practical changes do you need to make?

12. Think back over the whole letter. What reasons has Paul given you for shining with joy in your life? Which have most struck you and changed you, and why?

⊡ pray

Use your answers to Question Twelve to shape both your prayers of praise, and of petition.

Shining with joy
LEADER'S GUIDE

Leader's Guide

INTRODUCTION

Leading a Bible study can be a bit like herding cats—everyone has a different idea of what the passage could be about, and a different line of enquiry that they want to pursue. But a good group leader is more than someone who just referees this kind of discussion. You will want to:

- correctly understand and handle the Bible passage. But also…

- encourage and train the people in your group to do this for themselves. Don't fall into the trap of spoon-feeding people by simply passing on the information in the Leader's Guide. Then…

- make sure that no Bible study is finished without everyone knowing how the passage is relevant for them. What changes do you all need to make in the light of the things you have been learning? And finally…

- encourage the group to turn all that has been learned and discussed into prayer.

Your Bible-study group is unique, and you are likely to know better than anyone the capabilities, backgrounds and circumstances of the people you are leading. That's why we've designed these guides with a number of optional features. If they're a quiet bunch, you might want to spend longer on *talkabout*. If your time is limited, you can choose to skip *explore more*, or get people to look at these questions at home. Can't get enough of Bible study? Well, some studies have optional extra homework projects. As leader, you can adapt and select the material to the needs of your particular group.

So what's in the Leader's Guide? The main thing that this Leader's Guide will help you to do is to understand the major teaching points in the passage you are studying, and how to apply them. As well as guidance for the questions, the Leader's Guide for each session contains the following important sections:

THE BIG IDEA

One or two key sentences will give you the main point of the session. This is what you should be aiming to have fixed in people's minds as they leave the Bible study. And it's the point you need to head back toward when the discussion goes off at a tangent.

SUMMARY

An overview of the passage, including plenty of useful historical background information.

OPTIONAL EXTRA

Usually this is an introductory activity that ties in with the main theme of the Bible study, and is designed to "break the ice" at the beginning of a session. Or it may be a "homework project" that people can tackle during the week.

So let's take a look at the various different features of a Good Book Guide:

⊕ talkabout

Each session kicks off with a discussion question, based on the group's opinions or experiences. It's designed to get people talking and thinking in a general way about the main subject of the Bible study.

⬇ investigate

The first thing you and your group need to know is what the Bible passage is about, which is the purpose of these questions. But watch out—people may come up with answers based on their experiences or teaching they have heard in the past, without referring to the passage at all. It's amazing how often we can get through a Bible study without actually looking at the Bible! If you're stuck for an answer, the Leader's Guide contains guidance for questions. These are the answers to direct your group to. This information isn't meant to be read out to people—ideally, you want them to discover these answers from the Bible for themselves. Sometimes there are optional follow-up questions (see ⬆ in guidance for questions) to help you help your group get to the answer.

⊡ explore more

These questions generally point people to other relevant parts of the Bible. They are useful for helping your group to see how the passage fits into the "big picture" of the whole Bible. These sections are OPTIONAL—only use them if you have time. Remember that it's better to finish in good time having really grasped one big thing from the passage, than to try and cram everything in.

➔ apply

We want to encourage you to spend more time working at application—too often, it is simply tacked on at the end. In the Good Book Guides, apply sections are mixed in with the investigate sections of the study. We hope that people will realize that application is not just an optional extra, but rather, the whole purpose of studying the

Bible. We do Bible study so that our lives can be changed by what we hear from God's word. If you skip the application, the Bible study hasn't achieved its purpose.

These questions draw out practical lessons that we can all learn from the Bible passage. You can review what has been learned so far, and think about practical differences that this should make in our churches and our lives. The group gets the opportunity to talk about what they personally have learned.

⊡ getting personal

These can be done at home, but it is well worth allowing a few moments of quiet reflection during the study for each person to think and pray about specific changes they need to make in their own lives. Why not have a time for reporting back at the beginning of the following session, so that everyone can be encouraged and challenged by one another to make application a priority?

⬆ pray

In Acts 4 v 25-30 the first Christians quoted Psalm 2 as they prayed in response to the persecution of the apostles by the Jewish religious leaders. Today however, it's not as common for Christians to base prayers on the truths of God's word as it once was. As a result, our prayers tend to be weak, superficial and self-centred rather than bold, visionary and God-centered.

The prayer section is based on what has been learned from the Bible passage. How different our prayer times would be if we were genuinely responding to what God has said to us through his word.

1 Philippians 1 v 1-11
JOY-FILLED PRAYER

THE BIG IDEA
Our prayers should be fueled by love, joyful as we consider others' faith, and focused on their growth in Christian love. The highest goal in our lives and our prayers should be the glory of the God whom we serve, and in whom we enjoy grace and peace.

SUMMARY
This section of Philippians comprises:
- the greeting (or "salutation") in v 1-2, which reveals the writer as Paul, along with his young co-worker Timothy; and the recipients as the church in Philippi. Paul describes himself as (literally) a "slave" of Christ; and his readers as "saints" ("God's holy people," NIV) in Christ—those who have been set apart as holy. Philippi was a city in Macedonia (modern northeastern Greece); as a Roman colony, it was closely identified with Rome and its citizens were Roman citizens.
- Paul's reasons for thanking God for this church (v 3-8). Though Paul is in difficult circumstances—under house arrest in Rome—he is grateful for and joyful about the Philippian Christians, and therefore he is praying in thanks for them. He is convinced they are converted (v 5), and therefore is certain about their future (v 6).
- Paul's prayers for this church (v 9-11). Paul prays for their growth in love, with the chief aim that they might live in such a way as to bring glory to God (v 11).

OPTIONAL EXTRA
Before you begin, read through or listen to an audio recording of the whole letter to the Philippians. Ask your group each to think

about what they think the main themes or repeated ideas of the letter are. You could return to these answers at the very end of the final study, to see if your group would now add or change anything.

GUIDANCE FOR QUESTIONS
1. What do you think you can tell about someone from whether they pray, who they pray to, and what they pray?
Whether someone prays shows whether they accept they need help from a power other than, and greater than, theirs. *Who* someone prays to reveals their view of the divine (e.g. Christians are taught by Jesus to address their prayers to the God who is their "Father"). *What* someone prays shows the basis on which they relate to God (e.g. if someone prays, "God, I have obeyed you in this way and that way this week, and now I need you to help me in this way and that way," they reveal that they come before God on the basis of their own merits, and not on the basis of his kindness or mercy). It also reveals what and who they truly care about. Are all their prayers to do with themselves and their needs? If they pray for others, what do they ask for on their behalf?

2. What is notable about the way the writers of this letter—the apostle Paul and his co-worker Timothy—describe themselves (v 1)? As "bond-servants" (NASB)—translated "servants" in the ESV and NIV. This word—*doulos* in the Greek—actually means "slave." In the first century, a slave belonged to his master like a piece of property. He did not have a life of his own.

Further, a slave did not own anything. He was entirely dependent upon his master to meet all his needs.

Paul and Timothy present themselves as slave-leaders. Paul is an apostle, and yet also a slave of Christ, who has been bought by his master to be his possession.

- **How do they describe the recipients?** "All the saints in Christ Jesus who are in Philippi." "Saints" means "holy people;"; Paul is telling his readers that, negatively, a Christian has been set apart by God from their old life of sin and, positively is engaged to a new life of purity. Geographically his first readers are in Philippi. "Positionally" or spiritually, they are "in Christ Jesus." All that Christ is and all that he possesses belongs to them. The little phrase "in Christ Jesus" makes all the difference to everything.

EXPLORE MORE
Read Acts 16 v 6-40. Why did Paul go to Philippi (v 6-10)? Because the Holy Spirit so clearly directed them to preach the gospel there, preventing them from continuing on their course both to Asia and to Bithynia, and then sending a vision to Paul of a man from Macedonia (of which Philippi was the capital city).

Whom did God call to saving faith through Paul (v 11-34)?
- A wealthy business-woman named Lydia
- A demon-possessed slave girl
- A jailer

What do you think this taught Paul, and this new church, about:
- **who God can save?** Anyone. The first three members of the church were a successful, religious woman; a spiritually-oppressed, exploited girl; and a jailer (most likely an ex-soldier). None would have come to faith in Christ without God's work in them; but none were beyond his

powerful reach.
- **what circumstances God can work in?** God worked through Paul's prepared preaching at a place of worship, but also through his imprisonment in jail. God is always at work through his people in all circumstances—your group will see as they read through this letter that this was a lesson Paul knew well.

3. What is Paul doing, and how is he feeling (v 3-4)? Thanking God for the Philippians, and praying for them whenever he thinks of them. And he prays "with joy" (v 4).

- **Where is Paul as he writes (v 7, see also v 13-14)?** He is imprisoned. Verses 13-14 show us that Paul is under guard by the praetorian (imperial/palace) guard—he is in Rome, under house arrest.

- **How does this make his prayer and his emotion in verses 3-4 all the more striking?** As we read these words, we would never suspect that Paul was imprisoned. He is possessed with a triumphant joy. The tone of these words would lead us to assume that he must be attending a festival or celebrating with friends in their home. Who could imagine that he is, in fact, chained to soldiers, confined under house arrest?

4. What is the cause of Paul's joyful thanksgiving (v 5, 7)?
- v 5: The Philippian Christians' "participation/partnership in the gospel from the first day until now." They are involved together in a joint venture. Though separated by many miles, they remain in partnership together in being fishers of men and spreading the message of salvation to the world.
- v 7: The Philippian Christians are fellow

partakers/sharers of God's grace. Paul has strong feelings toward them because of their mutual salvation in Christ. What Paul feels for them is a deep-seated passion that has endured over the years. Like two pieces of metal welded together, his entire being is forged to them.

5. Why is Paul sure his Christian friends will keep going in their faith (v 6)?

Because it is God's work. This good work that God began in them commenced when the new birth made them alive in Christ. This points back to the time when Paul first preached the gospel in Philippi. God opened their hearts, and they believed the gospel. The apostle is convinced that what God began, God will complete. As believers in Christ, his readers are as certain for heaven as though they had already been there ten thousand years. God finishes what he starts.

• **Why is this confidence necessary for enabling him to pray with joyful thanks?** Paul's confidence that God will finish what he started means he does not need to worry about their salvation. He can simply enjoy it, and give great thanks for it. He can look forward to seeing them in eternity because he is confident that God has brought them to faith, and so he can be confident that God will keep them going in their faith (see 1 Thessalonians 2 v 19-20).

6. What impression of Paul do these verses give you?

He is a man of great love and tenderness. The virtue of loving people is what springs from each word of these verses. He is a grateful, joyful man. Regardless of the difficulties of the circumstances, others remain at the forefront of his mind and prayers. This is very different than the dry, doctrinaire, distant Paul that is the product of popular imagination.

7. APPLY: Given who Christ Jesus is and what he offers (v 2), why is it a privilege, rather than oppressive, to be one of his "bond-servants"?

Of course, to serve such a master—the Master who died out of love for his "bond-servants"—is neither restrictive nor an imposition. It is a privilege and a joy, for the great paradox is that such slavery brings true freedom—freedom from fear, futility and death. He is the one who offers "grace"—God's kindness in saving sinners and then giving them his Spirit to enable them to enter into a daily experience of his kindness; and "peace"—the supernatural experience of being at peace in your soul. To serve, or slave for, such a Servant-Master is freeing and fulfilling.

8. What does Paul's prayer in verses 9-10 teach us about what love in action looks like?

• We have already seen that Paul prayed for the Philippian Christians because he loved them. Prayer for others is love in action.
• Love seeks to "abound" in knowledge and discernment/insight (v 9). Genuine love never operates in a fog. Authentic love requires penetrating discernment into the real needs of people as they find themselves in real-life situations. It means having a heart understanding of people's lives that perceives their deepest needs and how we can best meet those needs.
• Love approves what is excellent / discerns what is best (v 10)—that is, it seeks to discern how best to love others. The challenge is often not in distinguishing between good and evil, but in deciding between what is good to do and what is best to do.

9. What does Paul's prayer teach us about what the purpose of the Christian

life is (v 11)? To live in such a way that we bring "glory and praise" to God. This chief end must be the supreme motivation for everything we do. Paul wrote to the church in Corinth, "Whether, then, you eat or drink or whatever you do, do all to the glory of God" (1 Corinthians 10 v 31). Such an all-inclusive statement means that all activity must be directed by this one master passion. A church's growing love for others will bring great praise to God.

10. So what is Paul teaching in verse 10 about what our aim must be as Christians? To live and love in a way that is sincere—to have a love that is real, so that when it comes into contact with the heat of a difficult situation or a difficult person that demands sacrifice or commitment, it does not melt away. Our aim must be to have a Christian character that does not crack under pressure.

Nothing must be hidden by the false cover-up of a religious façade. We must not appear to be one person on Sunday in church, but be someone else on Monday in our work. There must not be an inconsistency between what we confess to believe and how we live. Every area of life must fit together into a cohesive whole.

11. APPLY: How do the priorities of Paul's prayer here compare with our prayers? You might ask your group: How often do we pray, and how often does Paul pray? Who tends to be the focus of our prayers and of Paul's? How do we feel as we pray (if anything), and how does Paul feel? When we pray for others, what do we ask God to give them / do for them, and what does Paul ask?

Of course, in some areas and for some members of your group, their prayers will be similar to Paul's, and that is a matter of

encouragement. Where their prayers are not comparable to Paul's, that should be a spur to change.

- **If or where yours are different, what might this suggest about your view of God, or what matters to you in life?** If our prayers ask God for very little, it suggests we think God is capable of very little or willing to do very little.

If our prayers are infrequent, it suggests we think we do not need God's help very much.

If our prayers are for ourselves, it suggests we are self-centered.

If our prayers for others revolve around concerns of this world such as their career, health, wealth, etc., then it suggests that these are the things we most care about. (These are not bad things to pray about—but they should not be the primary focus of our prayers.)

12. APPLY: In what areas is your sincerity tested? What would an authentically loving Christian life look like when those tests come? Encourage your group members to discuss specific times when or areas where their conduct does not always match up with their Christian confession. Encourage them to see those tests as presenting them with an opportunity to pray for and live out a sincere love.

2 Philippians 1 v 12-30
JOY IN HARDSHIPS

THE BIG IDEA
To live is Christ and to die is gain—and so we can live with joy, whatever happens to us and whatever is said about us.

SUMMARY
Though Paul is imprisoned (v 13-14), and though there are those who, while Christians, are envious of Paul and are therefore preaching in such a way as to cause him trouble (v 15, 17), Paul is rejoicing. Why? Because his approach is to life that "to live is Christ" (v 21)—that is, his chief aim is to serve his King, to serve his people, and see his gospel proclaimed—and "to die is gain"—that is, if he is executed as a result of his impending trial before Caesar, he will go to be in the presence of Christ, which is "very much better" (v 23).

This is the approach Paul wants his readers to take to life, as he exhorts them to live in a manner which accords with their beliefs (v 27). V 27-30 show that to live for Christ means to stand firm, strive together, continue to believe, be willing to suffer for Christ, and so to continue in the "conflict" that is the Christian life in a fallen world.

OPTIONAL EXTRA
Show your group this picture—grand-illusions.com/opticalillusions/woman/. It is actually two images—the head of an old woman and also of a younger lady. Without saying there are two pictures, ask them what they see. Likely, some will see one; some the other. The point is that it is possible for people to see the same thing, but also to see things differently. Return to this after Q3 or 5 and point out that in Paul's situation,

many would see only the hardships—but he sees things very differently.

GUIDANCE FOR QUESTIONS
1. What makes you feel joyful? There is no need to seek a "right answer" at this point. Encourage your group to keep their answers concise.

- **What types of circumstances, or what actions of other people, can make you feel less good?** A lack of ... health, or freedom, or any sense of being in control, or sleep, or good relationships, etc; when we are criticized or deliberately worked against. Again, let your group share their own answers, briefly. You will return to the subject of this question in Q12.

2. What reasons does Paul have for not feeling good about life (v 12-17)?
- *His circumstances:* He is experiencing "imprisonment" (v 13, 14, 17). He is under house arrest (see Acts 28 v 30), confined to one small house as he awaits his trail before Caesar and the final verdict that will follow. He is being guarded by members of the praetorian guard (v 13)—the emperor's personal guards.
- *The actions of others:* Apart from those who have imprisoned him, there were those who were preaching the gospel because they were jealous of Paul. They were driven by "envy and strife" (v 15—rivalry, NIV)—and "selfish ambition" (v 17). They were attacking his reputation by casting doubt on his character—perhaps they were insinuating that Paul was in prison because God was punishing him ("If Paul were truly walking with the Lord,

he wouldn't be in prison"). They appear to have hoped to divide the church from Paul.

3. How is he responding (v 18)? Paul's response is utterly remarkable: "I rejoice." Even when thrown into prison, when others are turning against him, and when his good name is being slandered, Paul is rejoicing.

- **Why?**
- **v 12-13:** Because Paul's imprisonment has turned out "for the greater progress of the gospel" / "to advance the gospel" (v 12)— because he has shared the gospel with his guards, one on one. In turn, they, having eventually received the truth, have carried it into the palace of Caesar (see 4 v 22). Paul sees his confinement as a catalyst for the gospel to progress.

- **v 14:** The believers in Rome have far more boldness and courage to tell others about Christ. They see that Paul is willing to suffer for the gospel, and able to rejoice even when he has lost both liberty and security. Clearly, this example and challenge has exerted an enormous effect upon them.

- **v 18:** When people preach Christ out of a desire to cause trouble for him (v 17), nevertheless "Christ is proclaimed" (v 18—"preached," NIV). Paul is more concerned about the name of Christ going forward than rebutting his foes or escaping his suffering. It matters little what happens to him or what is said about him—as long as the Lord Jesus is glorified.

4. But what is he confident of (v 19-20)? That all that is happening "will turn out for my deliverance" (v 19), and that Jesus will be "exalted/honored" (v 20) in his body. Paul knows he will be released from his imprisonment, either by death or by release. And life and

death are both opportunities to serve the great end of advancing the name of Christ. He is confident not because he knows what the outcome of his trial will be, but because he knows and trusts the One who knows all things, who is with him, and who will bring him through death, whenever and however it comes.

⮟

- **If your group are unsure why Paul is so confident of his deliverance, ask: In what ways might Paul experience deliverance from his present circumstances?** Verse 20 suggests two options:
  1. By life—his release from prison.
  2. By death—his release from this life.

EXPLORE MORE
What are the gospel preachers whom Paul mentions in verses 15-17 motivated by? As we have seen, by envy, strife, and selfish ambition. Though they exalt Christ in their words, they use their ministry to promote and enrich themselves. They lift Christ up only in order to lift themselves up.
Read 1 Thessalonians 2 v 3-9. What was Paul's gospel proclamation motivated by? By a desire to please God, who cares about motives (v 4). By a love for others, who need to see and hear the gospel (v 8-9). It was not motivated by impure motives (v 3): a desire for popularity or money (v 5-6).
Read 1 Peter 5 v 1-4. What wrong motives could drive church leaders? A mere sense of duty (v 2); a desire to be enriched (v 2); a desire for control and power (v 3).
What right motives should drive church leaders? A desire to serve; aiming to be a good example to other believers of faith and

godliness (v 2-3); an anticipation of God's approbation in eternity (v 4).

What would bad motivations and godly motivations look like in your own life, in terms of your gospel proclamation and your serving within your church? A Christian's motives are critically important to God. It matters not only what we say and do, but why we do it. And all of us are susceptible to impure motives. So encourage your group to think hard about their own motivations for witnessing and serving.

5. APPLY: What prevents us from responding to difficult times as Paul did? Put simply, we have the wrong perspective on adverse circumstances and on difficult people. We rejoice in our comforts more than we rejoice about the name of Christ being advanced—and so when our comforts are removed, our sense of wellbeing and peace is too.

• **Think of a trial you have recently faced (or are facing now). What would it look like to respond in the same way as Paul?** Encourage your group to be specific, and to avoid making excuses as to why they cannot respond as Paul did, though of course their trial will be different in nature to his. Encourage them to maintain (or adopt) the perspective that God has placed us all in different circumstances with different trials in order to advance the gospel. If appropriate, pause at this point to pray to the Lord for one another.

6. What reason does verse 21 reveal for Paul's attitude in verses 12-20? Paul makes one of the most dramatic statements to come from his pen: "To live is Christ and to die is gain" (v 21—literally, it is "To live Christ, to die gain"). The passionate pursuit of his whole life is to know and glorify

Christ—everything is bound up with Christ. Therefore, as he sees the gospel being advanced despite (and in fact through) his adverse circumstances, his rejoices—because to live is Christ.

And Paul realizes that death will usher him to a much greater gain—the grave will graduate him to glory. He lives with the liberating knowledge that the best day of this life will be his last one. So he is not concerned about death. It will be "gain."

7. What is Paul's dilemma (v 22-26)? If his life is spared, he will be able to resume his ministry, which will be "fruitful" (v 22). But he would like to depart and be with Christ, which is far "better" (v 23). He is so excited about seeing his Lord face to face that being spared would almost be a disappointment!
Note: It is, of course, not really Paul's choice to make. The outcome rests in the hands of Caesar; and the matter is ultimately in the hands of God, who sovereignly controls the emperor's decision (see Proverbs 21 v 1). Paul is wrestling with the quandary of what to hope for. And he does not know which alternative to "choose."

• **What does he conclude is the best outcome and why?** That to remain is better, because it is "more necessary" for the sake of the church (v 24-25)—for the Philippians Christians' ongoing "progress and joy in the faith."
Notice that this is an act of self-denial on his part as he puts the needs of other believers before his own desires to "depart and be with Christ" (v 23).

8. How does Paul tell his readers to conduct their lives (v 27)? In a manner consistent with the gospel. They are exclusively to live in a way that matches and honors the gospel. They must model the message they have embraced. "Conduct yourselves" ("your manner of life," ESV) means to live as the citizen of a country in a law-abiding manner—Paul is saying that the Philippian believers are under an obligation to live in a way that is consistent with the word of God, which governs his people—those who are citizens of his kingdom. We must never be a walking contradiction between what we believe and how we act.

9. What words does Paul use in these verses to describe the faithful Christian life (v 27b-29)?
* *Stand firm* (v 27): Not being moved from their allegiance to the gospel.
* *Striving* (v 27): Obeying God's word requires effort (the word "striving" is the word from which we derive "athletic"), and it is to be done together.
* *Believe* (v 29): Saving faith is the beginning of the Christian life, and it is how we continue in it. It is a gift from God—he has "granted" it to us. No one can believe the gospel on their own. God made it possible for those who believe in him.
* *Suffer* (v 29): To all who are given saving faith, God also appoints suffering for his sake. The two gifts are inseparably bound together, and Paul speaks of suffering for the gospel, for Christ's "sake," as a privilege (see also 2 Timothy 3 v 12; 1 Peter 4 v 13-14). Suffering because of our salvation is to be expected and accepted.
* *Conflict/Struggle* (v 30): Literally, the word means "agony," like an athlete pushing themselves to the limit. For his readers, as for Paul, the Christian life was hard and painful. It was demanding, and it was never easy.

10. APPLY: The gospel is good news, but it is not easy news. How has Paul shown us this in verses 12-30? It is good news because it means we can say,

"To live is Christ and to die is gain." This gives us purpose in life and confidence in death. It means we view death as a good, not a disaster (v 23), and we can rejoice as Christ is proclaimed, no matter what our circumstances are.

But Paul has also shown us that the gospel is not easy news to live out. He has shown us primarily through his own example—Paul was imprisoned and maligned because of the gospel; he faced death because of the gospel—but also through the words he uses in verses 27-30 to describe the Christian life for us: standing firm, striving, believing, suffering, conflict.

11. APPLY: What goes wrong when we forget that...
* **the gospel is good news?** We will be joyless, and eventually we will likely give up on the Christian life, since it is hard to live as a Christian when there seems little purpose or point to the hardship.

* **the gospel is not easy news?** We will be complacent and we will not take our place in the fight together to contend for the gospel. We will be surprised by suffering or opposition. And death will be, in some measure, loss—the regret of missing the life we could and should have lived if only we had lived wholeheartedly for Christ, no matter the cost. Only if we do that will death be a graduation to glad glory when we stand before him.

12. APPLY: What have these verses shown us about how to live a joyful life? Refer back to Qs 2-3 and 6. If you have time, encourage your group to identify the times in their week when they will most need to say to themselves: "Christ is proclaimed; and in this I rejoice" (v 18), or "To live is Christ and to die is gain" (v 21).

3 Philippians 2 v 1-11, 19-30
JOY AND HUMILITY

THE BIG IDEA

Humility, as exemplified by Jesus in his incarnation and crucifixion, is a central tenet of the Christian life, and is to be pursued and highly regarded by all his followers.

SUMMARY

The Christian life is full of opposites that seem to contradict each other. Perhaps the greatest apparent contradiction is what we have before us in this chapter: we must humble ourselves if we are to be exalted.

"Humility" is a word that means to think or to judge ourselves with lowliness. The idea is for someone "not to think more highly of himself than he ought to think; but to think so as to have sound [or sober] judgment" (Romans 12 v 3).

This virtue of humility is the central theme that runs through 2 v 1-11, and again in v 19-30 (the intervening verses are the subject of the next study). The actual word "humility" is found in verse 3, but the concept is seen throughout this entire section. Paul calls upon the believers in Philippi to put on humility (v 3) as they carry out their ministry (v 4), in order to preserve their unity (v 1-2). In order to show us how to do this, the apostle will point to the Lord Jesus Christ as the supreme example in understanding true humility (verses 5-11).

Then in verses 19-30, Paul continues to show us what Christian humility looks like in the real lives of Paul's young son in the faith, Timothy (v 19-24), and Epaphroditus, a godly man who was the pastor of the church in Philippi (v 25-30), so that we can learn what authentic humility looks like.

OPTIONAL EXTRA

Find some fairly obscure words in the dictionary, split your group into teams, and ask them to come up with definitions (either accurate or hilarious) for each word. Lastly, ask them to define "humility." This leads into Q1.

GUIDANCE FOR QUESTIONS

1. What is humility? Encourage your group each to write down a one-sentence definition before sharing. There are no wrong answers at this stage—you might like to encourage your group members to return to review and possibly change their answer as they work through the study, particularly after Q4, 6, 9.

- **In what circumstances does your society celebrate humility? In what ways does it see humility as negative?** This depends on where you live, of course. But Western society tends to look upon humility as an abstract virtue but a real-life weakness. So we hear, "You need to back yourself" or "You've got to look after number one" or "Don't let people walk all over you" or "Sell yourself."

2. What do the Philippian Christians enjoy (v 1)?
- "Encouragement in Christ": The word "encouragement" literally means coming alongside another in order to help. Christ is with his people, to help them.
- "Consolation of love"/"comfort from his love": In the times of greatest discouragement, by his Spirit Jesus lifts up hearts and strengthens faith.
- "Fellowship of / common sharing in the

Spirit": This has the sense of a business partnership. The Philippian church are involved in the same venture, through the work of the Spirit.

- "Affection/tenderness and compassion": We should understand this as referring to the compassion of Christ. Christ loves his people abundantly.

3. If/since this is true of them, what does Paul appeal for (v 2-4)?

- Unity in love (v 2): The word "united" (NASB) here means "one-souled." They are to be welded together. Paul desires for them to stand as one body by making no distinctions among themselves. They must each love one another with the same love that they have for each and every member in their church.
- No acting out of "selfishness / selfish ambition" or "empty/vain conceit" (v 3): this is the kind of self-promoting attitude that creates, or even seeks and enjoys, divisions.
- "Humility" (v 3): The opposite of self-promotion, since it involves seeing others as more important than you. It is a mindset that calculates what would most benefit others, and then acts upon the result of that calculation. Naturally, we look out for our own "interests" (v 4). But Paul appeals to them to keep an eye out for others' needs just as much as they are for their own.

4. How do verses 2-4 define what it means to have "humility" of mind?

- Value unity above our own reputation.
- Love fellow members of the church, regardless of what they can do for us or how alike they are to us.
- Don't seek to use situations and areas of service for self-promotion.
- Rather, genuinely consider others as more

important than you.
- Therefore, seek to serve their interests before your own.

5. Why is Jesus the supreme example of humility (v 6-8)? Trace his journey from sovereign to slave:

- Jesus was fully God (v 6a). He has always existed, always in possession of all the divine perfections that belong to God alone.
- Jesus did not cling to or grasp at the full exercise of his divinity in order to serve himself (v 6). He obeyed his Father rather than standing on his rights.
- Jesus laid aside his prerogatives as God to take on the limitations of humanity (v 7)—to be a servant in human "likeness." **Note:** This does not mean Jesus emptied himself of his deity, or that he ever became less than fully God. Rather, he voluntarily chose not to exercise all his rights as God during this time on earth.
- Jesus was sufficiently humble that he died on a cross (v 8). He came into this world knowing that it would end with an ignominious death; not only that, but that he would submit to having the sins of his people laid upon him in his death, to bear their judgment.

Paul's point is that no one ever started so high and no one ever descended so low as Jesus, the Son of God.

- **How does this make verse 5 a great challenge to us?** Because we are to have the same attitude/mindset as Christ Jesus as we regard our time here in this world. The humility he displayed is our model. If he, the Son of God, lived this way, there is no reason or excuse for us not to. This is particularly challenging because our hearts struggle not to feel proud. Our default position is to exalt ourselves and look out for ourselves.

6. How did God the Father respond to the humility of God the Son (v 9-11)?

- He "exalted" him (v 9), giving him "the name which is above every name." Following his resurrection and ascension, Jesus was exalted to the Father's right hand, above the angels.
- God did this so that "at the name of Jesus every knee will bow" (v 10). God will ensure that everyone recognizes his authority and exalts him. Notice who bows: absolutely everyone.
- "Every tongue" will declare that "Jesus Christ is Lord." Every single person will confess the supremacy of Christ. This happens either at conversion, or at final judgment. In the end, Jesus will receive glory from everyone.

- **How does this encourage us to live with "humility" of mind?** The world may not notice humility (or look down upon it when it does notice it), but the point Paul is making in verses 9-11 is that no one ever truly humbles themselves before God without being exalted by God. True humility will never be forgotten by God. It is one thing to be exalted by man; it is something else entirely, and eternally, to be exalted by God.

EXPLORE MORE
Read Luke 18 v 9-14. How does Jesus teach here what Paul does in Philippians 2 about pride, humility, and exaltation?
The story is aimed at those who trust in their own righteousness, or moral goodness, and do so by comparing themselves with those whom they view with contempt (v 9). They are represented in Jesus' parable by the Pharisee, who is proud of his own comparative goodness and good deeds (v 11-12). The tax collector displays humility— he has a right sense of who he is, a "sinner," and a right sense of who God is

(hence he will not lift up his eyes to heaven, v 13). He also knows what he requires— mercy.
Jesus' point is the same as Paul's—those who exalt themselves now will be humbled by God one day, and those who humble themselves in the manner of the tax collector "will be exalted" by God.
What does this teach us about the link between our humility and our prayers?
Our prayers reveal our hearts. The Pharisee's prayer is full of pride because his heart is; he asks for nothing from God because he thinks he needs nothing from God; and he uses his prayer to pronounce his own goodness to God before men, so that they might notice him and praise him.
The tax collector's prayer is one of humble confession and humble request for mercy. If we have what Paul calls "humility of mind" (Philippians 2 v 2), our prayers will surely include a recognition of our sinfulness, our inability on our own merits to approach and enjoy God, and a request for his mercy, and great gratitude that in his grace he exalts repentant sinners.

7. APPLY: Think of some specific ways in which living with this kind of attitude would mean blessing for those around you in...
- **your church?**
- **your home?**
- **your workplace?**
Christ's humility brought blessing to his people, and will do so eternally. This question is designed to help you think about how Christ-like humility will positively affect the lives of those around you.

8. How does Timothy show us what humility looks like in real life (v 19-23)?
Humility is...
- *loyal:* Paul is in prison but Timothy is still by

his side (v 19).

- *loving:* Paul knows "no one else" who "will genuinely be concerned for your welfare" (v 20). Christians are not automatically like this; Paul knows many who are not (v 21). But Timothy is a living example of 2 v 4. We need to ask God to give us this same love for others—to care more for their welfare than our own comfort or reputation.
- *seen by others:* The Philippians know that Timothy is of "proven worth"/"has proved himself" (v 22). Timothy has been through hard times, and yet continued serving others. Humility will show itself in the way we treat and work for others.
- *hard-working:* "Served" (v 22) is better translated "slaved." Humility quietly puts in long hours, doing whatever is required for ministry to go forward and for people to be cared for. One example of Timothy's hard-working approach is the journey he is about to be given (v 19, 23).

9. Likewise, how does Epaphroditus show us what humility looks like in real life (v 26-27)?

- He is a soldier (v 25): Meaning, he is in the battle of spiritual warfare (see Ephesians 6 v 10-17). He is willing to step up and struggle hard.
- He is committed to encouraging others (Philippians 2 v 25): He gave up his comfort and convenience to travel to Rome from Philippi to seek out Paul and encourage him; now he is returning to encourage the Philippians.
- He cares more about the Philippians emotions than his own health (v 26-27): When he was at the point of death, his focus was not upon himself, but them. He was more concerned with how they were feeling about his illness than with the illness itself. This is a humble attitude.

10. How should the Philippian Christians think of and treat Epaphroditus (v 29)? They should rejoice to see him (as he brings this letter to them), and they should respect him highly. Humility is what should increase a believer's reputation within their church.

11. APPLY: Who is held "in high regard" (or "honored," NIV/ESV) in your church, and why? Would Timothy and Epaphroditus be? There are various good reasons for holding other believers in high regard—e.g. the way they parent their children in the gospel, their preaching or teaching gift, evangelistic heart, or faithfulness in suffering. But gospel-based humility should certainly be one reason. But because humility is by definition self-effacing, it is easy not to notice, or not to prize it.

12. APPLY: Do you find their examples more or less challenging than the example of the Lord Jesus? Why? Paul, in verses 6-8, presents Jesus as the supreme example of humility of mind lived out in action. Timothy and Epaphroditus are merely men who seek, imperfectly, to follow that supreme example. Yet Jesus, of course, is the sinless Son of God. It is possible to feel that we are not like him, and cannot hope to match him. But Timothy and Epaphroditus are not divine; they are mere men—just like us. In one sense, though their humility is imperfect, their example is more challenging, since we have no reason for not living like them. So there is no wrong answer to this question (some will find Jesus' example more challenging, others the example of these two men)—the purpose is to help conclude the study by reflecting on these three examples of humility, and how challenging each is.

4 Philippians 2 v 12-18
JOY IN OBEDIENCE

THE BIG IDEA
We are to work out our salvation by obeying God in each area of our lives, so that we might shine as lights in this world, holding out the gospel and rejoicing together.

SUMMARY
"Sanctification" means the divine act of making the believer increasingly holy on a practical level. This pursuit of holiness represents the lifelong process of making a person's moral condition come into conformity with their legal status before God of being "justified." Sanctification is God's continuing work in the believer, who is justified through the power of the Holy Spirit.

This next section is an important passage on this critical subject because it deals with the matter of spiritual growth over the duration of our Christian lives. Here we have the necessary balance in Christian living between our part (2 v 12) and God's part (v 13), followed by some specifics in how this will be evidenced (v 14-18), namely:
- not grumbling or disputing (v 14)
- shining distinctively as "lights/stars" (v 15)
- speaking the gospel to people (v 16— "holding fast" or "to" more correctly carries the idea of "holding forth")
- serving the church, as Paul did (v 17)
- sharing our joy (v 18)

Working out our own sanctification should bring great pleasure to us. It is restoring us to be the people we ought to be, and long to be. The truth that it brings pleasure to our Father in heaven is the reason why the fear and trembling within us (v 12) is joined with an inner pleasure and joy in the pursuit of godliness.

OPTIONAL EXTRA
To introduce the idea of shining as lights (or stars) through our distinctive, obedient lives, print out (or show on a screen) some famous constellations. Among those pictures, include one of the same sky, but in the daytime (when the stars are not visible because all is light) and a picture of a part of the sky where no stars are visible. Refer back after Q7 or 12. It is easy to forget the world is "dark." It is easy to know that it is, but still be the same as those around us. Paul is calling us to recognize the darkness of this sinful world, and to shine within it because we are different, obedient, joyful believers. Your church should be a glorious, bright-shining constellation!

GUIDANCE FOR QUESTIONS
1. What should a Christian aim to do in the time between being saved and going to heaven? There are an infinite number of possible answers, many of which are half-right:
- Wait
- Witness
- Hold on to your faith each day
- Help others

Explain to your group that we could sum up what a Christian should be doing this way: "Grow spiritually by growing in holiness"; or, to put it another way, "Be sanctified." This passage is one of the finest concise treatments of what that means in the entire Bible.

2. [Paul addresses these verses to Christians] With that in mind, what do you understand Paul to be saying in verse 12?

1. Obedience is important even though we are saved. When he says "always obeyed," Paul is not saying there has been perfect obedience, but that there is a habitual lifestyle of seeking to obey Jesus as Lord. Becoming a believer who is saved by grace does not negate our responsibility to keep the moral law of God. Salvation by grace must never be a reason for compromising our obedience to God.

2. We are to "work out" our salvation. Remember this is addressed to Christians— it is not about how to become a Christian or how to have eternal life. You may need to explain to your group that salvation in the Bible is represented in three different ways: past (when we were justified from the penalty of sin at the moment of conversion), present (when we are saved progressively from the power and practice of sin, in our ongoing sanctification) and future (when we will be saved ultimately from the presence of sin at the moment when Christ returns or takes us home to be with him, which will be our moment of glorification). Paul is speaking here of our present salvation. And Paul is saying that this process of salvation from the power/practice of sin will require "work"—we are commanded to put effort in. Growing as a Christian requires hard work—not to work for our eternal salvation, but to work out our salvation into each aspect of our lives, by obeying our Savior. (Linger on this point for a while if your group need to—it is vital to understand both what Paul is saying, and what he is not saying, by "work out your salvation."

3. Christians work out their salvation with "fear and trembling"; it is to be taken seriously. Q4 focuses on this in more detail.

3. Who is at work in the process of "sanctification"—that is, growing in holiness (v 12-13)?

- v 12: As you have seen in the previous question, we are.
- v 13: God is at work too.

God is always at work in his people, bringing about spiritual maturity. His work causes, empowers and enables our work. This does not undermine the need for us to work hard at obeying him, but it does mean that we are able to do it, since he is at work to help us. God works as we work, and we work because God works. (Remember, this is only true of the process of sanctification, of present salvation. Past and future salvation, or justification and glorification, are both only works of God—our efforts play no part at all.)

4. How does verse 13 explain why Christians obey "with fear and trembling"? What should our view of God be? "Fear" here (see dictionary on page 25) means healthy, reverential awe. Understanding who God is will produce in us an awe of him, and a seriousness about the work of sanctification. We will "tremble" because we know who is in us, working out our salvation with us. The idea is that a Christian will do their utmost to obey God because they know whom they are obeying. This is often downplayed today as a legitimate motive for Christian living, but it never was by Paul.

Note: How does living in "fear and trembling" fit with a letter that emphasizes the joy of Christian living? The gladness that believers experience grows out of the soil of fearing God with reverential awe. If we remember that God is a lion, not a teddy bear or a kitten, and that he is a lion who loves us, then we will know both the joy that such a God is for us and has saved us and the awe at who he is. We will avoid the temptation to domesticate him so that we view him merely as a kindly spiritual grandfather, sitting in the sky.

5. APPLY: What goes wrong in our Christian lives if we...
- **forget that we are called to work out our salvation, rather than work for our salvation?** We will be at risk of ceasing to trust in Christ for our past and future salvation, because we will look to our own efforts and deeds to achieve it. This is works-righteousness or self-justification, and it is opposed to the gospel. It will it will make us grow anxious (when we fail) and proud (when we think we are succeeding), and make us compromise on God's standards (in order to think we have met them). Most seriously, if it means we cease trusting Christ alone, it will mean that we are not Christians at all.
- **forget that God is at work?** We will likely grow complacent, as though God does not much mind what we do between here and heaven; or despairing, because the prospect of conquering sin and growing in holiness seems (and is!) too much for us to accomplish alone; or proud, because when God graciously works in or for us, we will attribute it all to our own efforts.
- **forget that we must be at work?** This is the approach of "let go and let God." But spiritual couch potatoes grow little in grace or holiness. Those who do not put much effort into sanctification make little progress in sanctification. (See Getting Personal below Q6.)

⊻
- **In how you live from day to day, which of these are you most in danger of forgetting? How would remembering it make a difference to you?**

6. APPLY: Why does a right view of God produce both joy and trembling? This first part of this question reinforces the point made in Q4, so see "Note" under that question. Make sure you also focus on the second part of this question...
How can we encourage each other to have this view? Let your group make suggestions. They may include:
- having it ourselves, so that we might set a good example!
- speaking of both our joy and our awe to one another.
- challenging other believers to take God seriously, especially in areas where they may not have seen they need to work hard at obeying God (of course, this must only be done with a humble attitude to ourselves and our own failings in this area—see Matthew 7 v 3-5).
- praying with others, in a way that is both full of awe and joy.
- asking for help. If you struggle to remember either that God is a lion, not a house-cat; or that he loves you and forgives yo,u and is not distant from you or angry with you—then ask other believers to remind you of the truth you struggle to remember, and to pray for you.

7. Why is verse 14 challenging? Because we are not to grumble or dispute/argue about anything. The word "grumbling" means private complaining under one's breath. Dispute is an attitude of continually questioning what is going on in the church. (This does not imply that a church member could never ask a question or raise a concern—the issue is the attitude of the heart and the tone of the voice.) How easy it is to fall prey to what Paul forbids here. It comes very easily to us to mutter and murmur about others, or to question everything our church leaders decide. And we are very quick to excuse doing it or to think it is not serious. But it is serious—it is disobedience.

- **How does verse 15 motivate us to obey verse 14?** Because grumbling and disputing prevent us becoming those through whom the light of Christ shines. As we live positively, we become "blameless" (this does not mean sinless, but being without obvious moral defect or blatant ethical blemish). And this means that we prove by the manner of our lives that we are genuine "children of God"— distinctive from those around us (for we live in a world where grumbling and disputing are very common, and almost expected). Paul pictures the Philippian Christians, as they grow in obedience, appearing "as lights in the world" (or, as the NIV translates it, they will "shine among them like stars in the sky"). So if we would have the light of Christ shine into the darkness from our church and our lives, we will need to grow in obedience and turn away from grumbling and disputing. That is how serious grumbling and disputing are.

8. What is the link between obeying verse 14 and being able to "appear as lights in the world, holding fast the word of life" (v 15-16)? If we are grumbling instead of joyful, we will not be distinctive—not be lights in the world. But if we are light in the darkness, then we will have opportunities to hold forth the "word of life." The way we live will provide the platform by which we are able to testify with our mouths. So we will have

many opportunities for our lips, instead of grumbling or arguing, to instead speak gospel truth to those around us.

9. How will Paul feel as he sees the Philippians working out their salvation and holding out the word of life (v 17)? He will "rejoice." He cares more for their salvation and sanctification than for his own freedom, or reputation, or wealth, because he knows that it is they who will be his joy in eternity (see Explore More for more on this).

- **How should the Philippians feel about it (v 18)?** They should rejoice too, sharing Paul's joy. Paul's reasons for joy should also be the Philippians' reasons for being joyful too. And Paul's joy should cause them to be joyful, while theirs will cause him to be joyful.

EXPLORE MORE
Read 1 Thessalonians 2 v 19 – 3 v 10. How does this passage give us further insight into:
- **how Paul feels about his Christian friends?** They are the cause of his joy and his exultation (2 v 19). His regard for them is so deep that he cannot bear not to have news from them (3 v 1-2, 5).
- **what Paul's priorities are for his Christian friends?** His greatest desire for them is not that they would avoid "afflictions/trials" (3 v 3). His priority is their ongoing faith (v 5)—and he cares so deeply about this that when he hears that they are continuing to trust in Christ, he can "really live" (v 8), since they "stand firm in the Lord." And Paul's prayers reflect this—he wants God to give them anything that they lack in their faith and understanding of how to live it out.
- **what Paul told young churches they could expect their Christian lives to involve?** Paul had warned them that

they were "destined" for "affliction/ persecution" (v 3-4).

10. APPLY: When do you find it easiest to grumble? How could you turn those moments into opportunities to praise God and hold out the word of life? Times of grumbling against others or about circumstances are also opportunities to increase in obedience to God, and shine more brightly in this world. Encourage your group both to be specific about how/when they grumble, and to be positive about how they can live and speak differently from now on.

11. APPLY: What have we learned is necessary for effective witness? Obedient lives, committed to working out our salvation—for instance, in ceasing to grumble and dispute—are crucial. If we do not live distinctively, we will not shine out and cause others to see glimpses of Christ's light.
But obedience is not sufficient—we must also speak gospel truth, communicating with our words the "word of life."
If we speak of the Lord without living for him, or live for him without speaking of him, then our witness will be ineffective.

• **How have you seen this kind of effective witness, either in your own life or in those around you?** Let your group's examples be of encouragement and challenge to each other.

12. APPLY: What have these verses shown you about how to shine with joy? We shine with joy as we grow in holiness. Our sanctification—and that of those we know—demonstrates that we/they are children of God, and that should be a cause of great joy to us, as it was to Paul. If we are not joyful, perhaps it is because we do not sufficiently value our own growth in obedience, or sufficiently care about the growth of others; or because we are not committed to working out our salvation at all. Those who are working it out, and know that God is working in them as they work, will be joyful people.

5 Philippians 3 v 1-21
JOY AS WE RUN

THE BIG IDEA
Authentic joy comes from having a personal relationship with God through Jesus Christ as we run our race with our eyes fixed on our future home with Jesus Christ.

SUMMARY
"Rejoice" (v 1) is a command to be obeyed. To rejoice in the Lord is the responsibility of every Christian to choose to obey.

But in Philippi, false doctrine was threatening to disconnect the Philippian believers from their source of joy in Jesus Christ. Judaizers were stealing the joy from God's people by putting them under the Old Testament Mosaic Law. They were teaching that to be saved, a person needed Christ-plus—trust in Christ *plus* something else—in this case, obeying Old Testament law in order to be saved.

False teaching always steals joy. Wrong teaching always leads to wrong thinking about God, which, in turn, always leads to wrong living—and to a lack of joyful assurance in salvation.

Paul uses his own testimony to show this. In verses 4-9, he states how his life was radically transformed from the inside out. Before he met Christ, he was doing many things, and was impressive in many ways—but he was not right with God. After meeting Christ, he lost many things, but he had all he needed—Christ.

And, having been converted, Paul had a new priority in his life—to know Christ (v 10); and a new power for his life—the power that raised Christ from the dead.

So Paul now runs hard for home with Christ

(v 12-14). He is forgetting the past, with all its failures and defeats. With an all-absorbing effort, Paul is reaching forward to the finish. He will "press on toward the goal for the prize of the upward call of God in Christ Jesus" (v 14). This must be the "attitude" (view/thinking) of every Christian (v 15).

Lastly in this section, Paul directs the attention of the Philippians upward to their heavenly home. False teaching would have us live for the present and lose our joy about our future (v 18). But, "our citizenship is in heaven, from which also we eagerly wait for a Savior, the Lord Jesus Christ" (v 20). In the first century Roman world, "citizenship" was sometimes bestowed on a colony or city, despite its people being born outside, and very possibly never having visited, the country of which they were citizens. Paul is reminding the Philippian Christians that even though they live in the Roman colony of Philippi, their real citizenship is in another place. Their names are permanently recorded where the King of kings, Jesus Christ, is enthroned at the right hand of God. So they (and we) must keep running joyfully, as they "eagerly wait" with great expectation for Jesus Christ to bring them to heaven or return to them from heaven.

OPTIONAL EXTRA
Find footage of an Olympic or World Championship sprint with a close finish. Discuss together what makes a good sprinter—it includes natural physique and training, but also the ability to execute the race (to keep your knee-lift high and stride long, maintain relaxed shoulders, dip for the line, etc) Explain that Paul uses this as a

picture of the Christian life, as we shall see in this study.

GUIDANCE FOR QUESTIONS

1. Imagine you had to spend a year outside of your own country. What do you think you would most miss about it? What would you most look forward to as you thought about returning? We do not necessarily belong where we live. Christians do not—our "citizenship is in heaven" (v 20). In this study, your group will see how this citizenship should bring us joy and should mean we live differently than those around us. You could return to this question at the end of the study, but ask your group what they are most looking forward to about reaching the country where they are citizens—God's eternal kingdom.

2. What is the command in verse 1? What difference does it make that it is a command, not merely a request or encouragement? "Rejoice in the Lord." Do not miss the challenge that we are commanded to rejoice. Paul's readers may not have felt like rejoicing, but that did not give them an excuse to mope around. That would be to disobey God. Believers are to rejoice in the Lord, always. The next verses (and the previous chapters) give us reasons to rejoice about our relationship to him— God does not command what he does not make possible.

3. What do you think Paul means when he talks about putting "confidence in the flesh" (v 3-4)? "The flesh" refers to a person's own ability, independent of God. Paul is referring to anything that someone does that is independent of trusting in God. It is anything that you and I might do apart from a reliance upon the power of the Holy Spirit, either to earn or keep salvation or blessing. It is anything we rely on alongside or instead of Christ—a Christ-plus approach to our salvation. **In what way are the "dogs" (false teachers) doing this (v 2)?** These false teachers are the "false circumcision / mutilators of the flesh," which explains what they teach and impose upon others. The religious rite of male circumcision was taught in the Old Testament as a sign of God's covenant with the nation of Israel (Genesis 17). The death of Christ fulfilled the meaning of circumcision (Colossians 2 v 10-14). But these Judaizers were attempting to keep people under the old covenant by requiring their followers to be circumcised. It was Christ-plus teaching.

- **How would such a view of life pollute Christian joy?** They stripped the gladness out of their followers by putting them under the Old Testament Mosaic Law. Fulfilled in Christ, however, the act of circumcision was no longer binding upon the believers in Philippi. This requirement of circumcision and other such rules placed heavy demands upon the people. If salvation relies on Christ's finished work, then we can enjoy knowing he has accomplished it. But if it relies on our work in any way—here, by obeying Old Testament law—then we will always be anxious, wondering whether our performance has been sufficient. And anxiety and joy cannot co-exist.

4. What did Paul place his confidence in:
- **before his conversion (v 4-6)?**
- *Impressive beginning.* He was "circumcised the eighth day" (v 5). The Mosaic Law required that on the eighth day, a baby boy would be circumcised, which was the cutting of the male foreskin and the sign of the covenant. Paul had been.
- *Impressive nationality.* He was born "of the

nation/people of Israel" (v 5). Israel was God's chosen nation, and they were the people who were privileged to hear the word of God preached to them. No other nation had such an advantage through access to the word of God.

- *Impressive lineage.* Paul was "of the tribe of Benjamin" (v 5). Of the twelve tribes of Israel, Benjamin was one of the two elite tribes. They were one of the two tribes that remained loyal to King David's descendants when the kingdom divided; together, they formed the southern kingdom of Judah.

- *Impressive upbringing.* Paul was "a Hebrew of Hebrews" (v 5). That is to say, he was born of Hebrew (that is, Jewish) parents and was raised according to Hebrew tradition. He was reared in a Hebrew home and learned the Hebrew language. No one could be any more Hebrew than Paul was.

- *Impressive standard.* "As to the Law [Paul was] a Pharisee" (v 5). The Pharisees were those men most committed to the Old Testament Scriptures. They were Scripture-believing, Scripture-reading, Scripture-studying, Scripture-teaching, Scripture-preaching people.

- *Impressive sincerity.* "As to zeal, [Paul was] a persecutor of the church" (v 6). Paul was not lukewarm about anything he did. He was filled with sincerity, so much so that not only did he love what he believed to be right, but he hated what he was convinced was wrong. From this character came his violent persecution against the church of the Lord Jesus Christ.

- *Impressive morality.* Paul was "blameless/faultless" when it came to obeying the law (v 6). Had we been there, we would have stood back and looked at the life of before-conversion Paul, and concluded that here was a straight arrow if there ever

was one. He was outwardly moral. He was extremely upright.

If anyone could have ever earned their way to heaven by their own religiosity, Saul of Tarsus would have been number one, and at the head of the line.

- **after he turned to Christ as his Lord (v 7-11)?** Paul describes his conversion in the style of an accountant looking at a profit-and-loss statement. "Whatever things were gain to me" (everything he listed out in v 4-6) he moved from the asset side to the liability side—he counted them "as loss" (v 7). Paul now saw them as that which would condemn him—not because they were negative in themselves, but because they were a bad debt when he arrogantly trusted them to secure him entrance to heaven.

Now his confidence is in "the surpassing value/worth of knowing Christ Jesus my Lord" (v 8). He is saved by the Christ whom he knows personally—not by anything he does or is. His righteousness—his right standing before God—is not based on his obedience of the law but through "faith in Christ" (v 9). He relies on "the power of His resurrection," rather than on his own natural abilities. He is confident even in suffering, for he knows that he is suffering for Jesus' sake, and will also share in his resurrection (v 10-11). Paul's confidence for his salvation, righteousness, life, and future is all in Christ Jesus, compared to whom he sees all things as loss/garbage (v 8).

EXPLORE MORE
Read Acts 9 v 1-18. Why was Saul/Paul traveling to Damascus (v 1-2)? To arrest the Christians he found there, drag them back to Jerusalem and have them stand trial, with the hope of putting them to death. **What happened to change his plans,**

and his life? A light—the glory of God, the very presence of the living God—shone round him. From it, Jesus spoke to him. Saul/Paul realized that this was the "Lord."

How does Jesus characterize what Saul/Paul was seeking to do to the church (v 4)? Jesus says that Saul is "persecuting Me"—to persecute the church is to persecute the head of the church, the Lord Jesus Christ. To come against the church of Christ is to come against Christ himself.

What does this episode, unique though it is, reveal generally about Christian conversion?

• Every conversion occurs at a moment (even when there is a process leading up to it) when we cross the line.

• Conversion involves confessing the Lordship of Christ.

• Christ is the great initiator of every conversion. Saul was not looking for Christ; neither is anyone (see Romans 3 v 11). We were not looking for God, nor did we find him; he looked for us and found us. See Ephesians 2 v 1-6.

5. APPLY: In what kinds of ways do we see the same Christ-plus false teaching in our day that Paul saw in Philippi? Any approach to life and faith that preaches or believes that we must do more in any way than believing in Christ is Christ-plus, and it robs us of joy and salvation. Let your group discuss the kinds of Christ-plus teaching they have heard of or experienced. One example of such false teaching is the false doctrine that teaches that water baptism, whether of infants or of adults, is necessary for salvation. Such teachers teach that church membership is necessary for salvation. They teach that last rites, or the acquiring of indulgences, is necessary for salvation.

• **Is Paul right to call such teachers "dogs"? Why/why not?** This reference

is not to a domesticated house pet, but to wild scavengers. Paul is saying that these false teachers are like vicious wild dogs that roam the streets in packs from one garbage dump to the next, devouring what has been thrown away; who attack innocent people and spread disease. This is an extremely strong description; but think about what false teachers are doing. They are ravaging people by selling them falsehood as truth, by pulling them away from or preventing them coming to true faith, through a clever perversion of what the Bible teaches. They rob people of salvation. Paul is right to call anyone who adds to salvation by grace alone, through faith alone, in Christ alone, a "dog." When we are too soft on false teaching and those who peddle it (rather than those who are duped into following it), it is because we do not consider the seriousness of the eternal implications of what they are doing.

6. APPLY: Imagine someone in your church has just been bullied in their workplace or has lost their job because of their loyalty to Christ. How do these verses teach you to encourage them?

• Whatever they have lost, their confidence for salvation or life was not in that anyway—they still know Christ, and their eternity is unaffected.

• Following the Christ who suffered will involve suffering for him—that is what they have experienced. It is not pleasant, but it is also not surprising.

• Because they know the Christ who gives them righteousness, they can still rejoice, even though their circumstances have grown worse.

7. How does Paul now view his past, his present, and his future (v 12-14)?

- *His past:* He forgets "what lies/is behind" (v 13), with all its failures and defeats.
- *His present:* He is resolved to "press on" (v 14). Paul has not arrived—there is still much growth for him to realize and much for him to do. He aims to run hard, because he knows what lies ahead.
- *His future:* Paul reaches forward toward the finish—the "prize" of being with Jesus, and like Jesus, in heaven (v 14).

- **How do verses 20-21 excite believers about "what lies ahead"?** In the first century Roman world, "citizenship" was sometimes bestowed on a colony or city, despite its people being born outside, and very possibly never having visited, the country of which they were citizens. Paul is reminding the Philippian Christians that even though they live in the Roman colony of Philippi, their real citizenship is in another place. Their names are permanently recorded where the King of kings, Jesus Christ, is enthroned at the right hand of God. And he will return to bring his citizens to his kingdom. At his triumphant return, Christ "will transform the body of our humble state into conformity with the body of His glory" (v 21). This dramatic appearing will alter not only the souls and spirits of believers, but also our frail bodies. Right now, our bodies are in a "humble state/lowly," subject to the weaknesses, diseases, and death of this world. But when Jesus returns, our bodies will be made like his resurrected, glorified body. We will have a heavenly body perfectly suited for our new environment. We will be enabled to worship and serve Christ throughout all eternity and never grow weary in our new, eternal occupation in the country we call home. In that final state, our worship will be made perfect. This prospect produces the eager anticipation that all citizens of heaven can and should have.

8. How does Paul want his readers to respond to his words?
- **v 15:** To have the same attitude toward our past, our present, and our future as he does (see Q7). Right thinking is foundational to right living.

- **v 16:** To carry on living by "that same standard" we have "attained" (NIV obscures this slightly). "Keep living/hold true to/live up to" has the sense of soldiers marching in a row—to keep in step with what is required: obedience to the word of God. We must carry on staying in step with the truths that we have been taught (which will also involve rejecting new teachings—false teachings).

- **v 17:** To follow Paul's example, and the example of those who live in the way that he does. Paul wants his readers to focus their attention upon other godly examples who model authentic Christ-likeness—to note and replicate the pattern they set. Refer your group to the Getting Personal section under this question in the Study Guide.

9. What are the alternative future and present that the "dogs" would lead this church into (v 19)? Paul minces no words. The end of this road is "destruction," or eternal damnation.
"Appetite/stomach/belly" refers not to their physical hunger, but, metaphorically, to their sensual lusts. They worship what feels right, or what feels good. Their own desires are elevated to the level of divine authority in their lives. Further, their "glory is in their shame." This likely describes the false teachers' self-boasting, in which they glory in themselves. They elevate themselves in their own eyes before others.

10. APPLY: What are the appetites that your culture seeks to satisfy, that lead to shame and destruction? Encourage your group to think about their own culture, not others (it is always harder to spot the false promises and gospels that are closer to us than those that are further away). One answer might be wealth and possessions—the idea that the more we have, the happier we will be, and/or the more blessed by God we must be. **Of those, which do you think are most likely to seep into the way Christ's people live within your culture?** For some this might be the "prosperity gospel" of "name it, claim it" teaching—a get-rich-quick scheme under the supposed guise of Christianity, which panders to the appetite for wealth. Such materialism can creep into the approach to life even of those who reject the more overt forms of the "prosperity gospel." But again, encourage your group to think about themselves, and your own church.

11. APPLY: How can you help one another to run hard for home? In various ways—but at the least, it will involve remembering your answer to Q6, and encouraging one another to have the same view of the past, the present and the future that Paul did.

12. APPLY: What truths have given you cause for joy during this study? How will you remember them, and remind others of them? This question aims to sum up the study and link its truths back to the command in verse 1 to "rejoice."

6 Philippians 4 v 1-9
JOY WHEN FACED WITH CONFLICT AND ANXIETY

THE BIG IDEA

Conflicts within the church need to be met with joy, and are overcome by remembering our gospel unity. Anxiety in our hearts needs to be met with joy, and is overcome by praying with thanks and trust.

SUMMARY

Conflict is too often found in the church of Jesus Christ. The church in Philippi was no different. There were two women at the heart of a brewing storm. Paul urged these two women to live in harmony. This was not a small feud in this church, but a major problem threatening its strength and witness. This conflict was not theological, but relational.

At this time, it is a challenge to rejoice. But the church is nevertheless commanded to do so (v 4). These in-house differences and disagreements should not prevent the Philippians from rejoicing. Most likely, rejoicing together may serve to heal the divide. Rejoicing in all the Lord is to us and for us will tend to correct our perspective on everything else, especially in conflict.

Paul moves on from conflict to anxiety. Again, he gives a command: "Be anxious for nothing" (v 6). Though it may be strange to think of it like this, to be anxious is to be disobedient to God; it is the failure to believe the promises of God in his word.

Jesus taught the same, as the Explore More section shows: "Do not be worried/anxious about your life…" (Matthew 6 v 25).

There is, Paul says, one primary cure for worry, and that is dependent prayer (Philippians 4 v 6): we are to bring our concerns about what we lack to the Lord. We should trust that God will answer the prayer and meet our need according to his perfect will. And we are to pray with "thanksgiving"—at the same time as recognizing what we lack, we must also acknowledge what God has provided for us.

The promise in this is that taking our concerns to God in prayer brings his abundant, supernatural peace (v 7). In order to enjoy that peace, we must also focus our minds upon those things that are worthy of our thought (v 8). Dependent prayer and purity of mind are the essentials for peace of heart.

OPTIONAL EXTRA

Listen together to a piece of orchestral music, played by a symphony orchestra. Identify as many different instruments as you can. Discuss how much effort is required to make a piece of music sound apparently effortlessly beautiful. Discuss what would happen if one musician played some discordant notes. The point is that it would affect not just them or their section, but the performance of the whole orchestra. So it is with churches, and with conflicts in churches—they affect the whole peace of the church, and its witness. Hence the importance Paul attaches to the resolution of the conflict he mentions in these verses.

GUIDANCE FOR QUESTIONS

1. For what kinds of reasons do Christians who are members of the same church fall out with one another? For the same reasons non-Christians do. Ever since Cain and Abel (Genesis 4 v 1-16), there has been conflict between individuals. Wherever there are sinful people, there is the potential for conflict. You could read James 4 v 1-4 to your group. **Does it matter?** Yes. Conflict can threaten the effectiveness of the church's ministries, and it always undermines the unity of Christians, which is part of the mission of Christ (see Ephesians 2 v 11-22). Consequently, whenever conflict arises in the church, it must be properly addressed and rightly resolved.

- **For what reasons do Christians worry? Does it matter?** Again, it seems natural to worry. Christians worry about the same things non-believers do, and for the same reasons—they are not in control, or feel they lack capacity to do what is needed. The difference (as you will see in the study) is that Christians are commanded not to worry—worry is the failure to believe the promises of God in his word. So it matters very greatly—not only is worry robbing us of our joy, but it is disobedient to our Lord.

2. What appears to be the problem Paul is addressing (v 2)? Two women, Euodia and Syntyche, are at odds with one another. This squabble was serious enough that Paul incorporated it into this short letter of only four chapters.

3. What are we told about Euodia and Syntyche in verse 3? How does this underline the seriousness of what is happening within this church? They were well-known members of this congregation, and fellow workers with Paul in the gospel.

These were not obscure members in the life of this flock. These were frontline warriors—two servants who had put their shoulders to the plow in the cause of the gospel. The problem was not that they were not involved in God's work, but that they were not united with one another as God's people. This is why it is particularly serious—this is a conflict between converted, committed members of the church. It therefore has the potential to affect the unity of the entire church. The friction between these two may disrupt the spiritual life of those around them and fracture the fellowship of the church.

4. What commands and truths does Paul give in this situation, and who to? For each, consider how this command and/or truth would help the reconciliation of these women and resolve the conflict.
- **v 1:** The command is to the whole church to "stand firm." They are not to compromise and either soft-pedal truth, or downplay the seriousness of unity among themselves. And they are to stand firm "in the Lord"—they must rely on the Lord for all things in all situations.

- **v 2:** The command comes to the two women to live in harmony as Christian sisters. Paul here is showing how important their harmony and unity is to him, and to the rest of their church. They are both addressed—both have the responsibility to seek peace. Notice harmony must be "in the Lord"—their shared faith must be their common ground. If they are right with God, then they can become right with each other once more.

- **v 3a:** Paul asks his "true companion" to help the feuding pair. He clearly has a particular member of the church in view—

in fact, "true companion" (*Syzygos*) is likely this person's name, not a description of them. Paul knows that in conflicts, very often a respected third party needs to help bring harmony.

- **v 3b:** A truth—these women's names are "in the book of life." Conflict does not mean they are unconverted. Paul is again reminding the two women that they have far more in common than divides them.

- **v 4:** The church is commanded to "rejoice." Such a dispute can make rejoicing seem impossible. However, Paul urges the believers to rejoice nonetheless. Most likely, rejoicing together may serve to heal the divide. Rejoicing in all the Lord is to us and for us will tend to correct our perspective on everything else, especially in conflict (see Getting Personal section after Q5).

- **v 5a:** There is a command to be gentle. Emotions must not be allowed to escalate and intensify when conflict rises up. In such times, level-headed responses are called for from others in the church.

- **v 5b:** "The Lord is near/at hand." This is not a statement concerning the second coming of Christ. Rather, this is an affirmation that the Lord is near to his people in order to give his joy to troubled hearts. The Lord is present as reconciliation between these two disputing women is sought. This is a simple reminder of Christ's closeness to his people in a time of unrest, to grant his peace and to calm hearts.

5. APPLY: Imagine Euodia and Syntyche are in your church. What has this passage taught you about how you need to respond?

- You need to stand firm in the gospel and keep living as a Christian.

- You need to consider becoming proactively involved in resolving the dispute, rather than ignoring, excusing or belittling it; and, if it is not for you to do so, you need to pray for those who are seeking to resolve it.
- You need to rejoice in the Lord even while living through the conflict.
- You need to speak gently to and about the issue, rather than resort to gossip, anger or criticism.

- **Imagine that you are Euodia or Syntyche. What has this passage taught you about how you need to respond? How has it motivated you to obey?** You need proactively to pursue peace, and accept others' help in doing so. You can be motivated by remembering that this really matters—you are undermining the unity of the fellowship; that God is near to help; and that whatever divides and upsets you is far exceeded by what you have in common with a fellow believer, for your names are both in the book of life. Those who will spend an eternity in joyful unity ought to start living in it now.

6. What is the cure for anxiety, according to verses 6-7?
There is one primary cure for worry, and that is prayer. In this context, these prayers address whatever is causing the anxiety and stealing our peace of mind. Notice the stark contrast between "nothing" and "everything" (or "anything" and "every situation")—a believer is to be anxious for "nothing," but praying about "everything." "Everything" carries the idea of every troubling situation that threatens the peace of God in us.

So we need to ask ourselves: What has been weighing me down? Here is the ground where anxiety will flourish, if unchecked and unchallenged. But this also is the ground where dependence, trust and joy may grow, if we pursue dependent prayer.

7. What difference does it make that the beginning of verse 6 is a command, and not an aspiration? It means that acting upon Paul's words here is not optional. It is an obligation. This forces us to ask why. It is because (though it may be strange to think of it like this) to be anxious is to be disobedient to God. Worry is a failure to trust that God is in control. It reveals that we are not sure that God will provide what we need in his perfect timing. Worry is gazing at my problems in self-reliance or self-pity or both, rather than looking to the Lord in dependence. Worry is the failure to believe the promises of God in his word.
Note: This does not mean that we should not be concerned about issues in our lives in the midst of difficulties. Yet Paul stresses that believers must not be pulled apart and robbed of peace and joy—we must not be anxious and worried.

- **God never commands what he does not enable. What truths in verses 5-7 enable us to obey this command?** The Lord is near (v 5)—he is able and willing to help us. He is in control. When we panic, heaven does not. God has plans to work out his good purposes in our lives, and when we pray, we are recognizing that we are dependent upon him, and that we can trust him.
The result of casting our burdens on the Lord is that we are unstressed and undisturbed; or, as Paul says, we know a peace that "surpasses all comprehension / transcends all understanding" (v 7)—that is, it exceeds human explanation.

EXPLORE MORE
Read Matthew 6 v 25-34. What does Jesus command his followers not to do, and to do?
- **v 25:** Do not be worried about what you will eat, drink, or wear.
- **v 31:** The command not to worry is repeated.
- **v 33:** Seek as your priority the interests of God's kingdom, and the life of righteousness (that is, Christ-likeness).
- **v 34:** Again, the command is to not worry.
What truths does he remind us of, to enable us to obey his commands?
- **v 25:** There are often more important things than those that we worry about. If you are in Christ, you have eternal life, and that is far more important than what you eat, drink, or wear.
- **v 26, 30:** God cares for his creation; and humans are the pinnacle of his creation, and more valuable to him than birds or fading flowers. Since he cares for his creation, we can be sure he cares about us.
- **v 27:** Worrying does not work. It does not change the day of our death.
- **v 32:** God is our Father—he loves us and looks out for us, and he knows exactly what we need. We do not need to worry that we will be left without what we need to walk on in faith until we are home with our Father. We do not need to worry that we are missing out in some way.
- **v 33:** As we focus on his kingdom and living rightly, we can be confident that he will take care of the details of our lives, for our good and his glory.

8. How can we actively "dwell on" or "think about" Paul's list in verse 8? Work through the list and think about what kinds of thoughts are being promoted here (there is some overlap between the words—Paul's concern is with the totality of our thoughts):
- True: that is, what Scripture says
- Honorable/noble: things that help us to

live morally

- Right: that which matches up with God's holiness
- Pure: clean, wholesome
- Lovely: sweet, generous—thoughts which are beautiful to God
- Of good repute/admirable: respectable in the eyes of God and his people
- Excellence/excellent: actively seeking to think as well as we can; not settling for spiritual mediocrity
- Worthy of praise/praiseworthy: again, the idea here is to ask, "Can this thought be praised by God?"

9. What do you think would be the opposite of obeying verse 8? As you work through, encourage your group to think of particular things their minds could dwell upon that would be in one way or another the antithesis of Paul's command here.

10. APPLY: [There is an inseparable connection between what we think about and how we live.] How have you experienced this, both positively and negatively, in your life? The aim of this question is to help us realize that what we think about matters. We are often surprised by a wrong action that we see in someone else, or in ourselves—but we can be sure that such an action was preceded by a thought life that, because it was unchecked, led to that outward sin. We are all too ready to excuse our impure, unholy thoughts. So we need to recognize that they matter to God, and also that they are reflected in our actions.

11. APPLY: What has this passage taught us are three great dangers to joy and peace?
1. Conflict within a church

2. Anxiety inside a Christian
3. False and unholy thoughts inside our minds

- **How can you encourage one another to avoid these pitfalls and so enjoy "the peace of God" (v 7)?** Encourage your group to work through these three dangers and come up with specific answers. The first will have been covered at least in part by Q5. For worry, we need not to excuse each other's worry, but to encourage and, when necessary, challenge fellow believers to pray, and to leave their worries with the Lord. And we need to ask one another about our thought lives and, when we are struggling with sin, to ask each other for help and prayer; or, when we are counseling someone who has sinned, we should help them see that the battle against sin begins with the battle of the mind. And in all this, we need to be reminding each other that peace and joy are the great results of living wholeheartedly for the Lord in unity, in prayer, and in our thoughts.

7 Philippians 4 v 10-23
JOY IN ALL THINGS

THE BIG IDEA
Real contentment comes from relying on Christ to enable us to obey him, and not from our circumstances. One fruit of this contentment is joy-filled, sacrificial financial giving.

SUMMARY
As we consider Paul's words in verses 10-13, we need to remember that his circumstances are anything but good. The apostle is imprisoned in Rome, chained to the elite Roman guards who serve in Caesar's household. He is awaiting trial before Caesar with his own life at stake, confined under house arrest, and unable to move about with freedom.

Yet Paul is "content" (v 11). He is a man who is content despite his circumstances, rather than being crushed by them.

Here is the reason for his contentment: he is grateful that God has met his needs through the generosity of the Philippians (v 10); but, more than this, he has "learned" how to be content in both adversity and prosperity.

To be content is to have a peaceful acceptance of where God has providentially placed you. And it comes from knowing that "I can do all things through Him who strengthens me" (v 13). "All things" refers to all things within the will of God—all things that glorify God. Paul is saying (and showing how we may say), *I am content no matter what my circumstances are. I can get along with little, and I know how to live with much. I am content whether I am full or hungry, wealthy or in need. I can do all things through my Lord, who strengthens me.*

In verses 14-23, Paul concludes with an expression of gratitude for the ministry partnership that he continues to maintain and enjoy with the Philippian Christians. He states his thankfulness for their financial help during these trying times. Finally he ends with a doxology of praise for God and final greetings to the believers in Philippi.

The study picks up on Paul's words about financial giving. The apostle uses the imagery of an Old Testament sacrifice being offered by the priest on the altar (v 18). In this act, incense was poured onto the sacrifice, releasing a fragrant aroma that ascended upward to heaven. The sweet-smelling fragrance pictured the pleasure that such a sacrifice brought to God. In like manner, the giving of the Philippian Christians is an expression of their worship of God that is well-pleasing to him. Here is the ultimate purpose and the greatest motive for our financial giving to gospel ministry. And such giving will flow from a heart which finds its contentment and joy not in prosperity, but in Christ.

OPTIONAL EXTRA
Whether or not you did this at the start of Study One, either at the beginning or end of this study read through or listen to an audio recording of the entire letter to the Philippians.

GUIDANCE FOR QUESTIONS
1. If there were one thing you could change or add to your life to make you more content, what would it be? Most of us take the view that a change in our circumstances—perhaps a relationship, or

greater financial power, or a promotion in our career, or a larger house, or more children or older children or younger children, and so on—would mean that we enjoy a greater sense of contentment. Share your own "one thing" here, so that your group do not feel that you are not struggling with the same impulse to look to circumstances for contentment. As you go through the study, you will see how Paul is content despite his circumstances, not because of them.

- **What role do circumstances and wealth have to play in making us feel content in life?** This underlines what will likely have been revealed by the previous question. In the way we naturally view life, circumstances and wealth are the deciding factors in our contentment.

2. What is Paul joyful about (v 10—verse 18 gives more detail on what Paul is referring to here)? He is grateful that the Philippians have revived their "concern" for him, seen in their financial gift to him, which Epaphroditus has delivered from them (v 18). But notice that Paul is not joyful because he now has more money, but because he now knows that the Philippians are concerned from him, in gospel love and partnership with him.

3. Was his joy and contentment dependent on this assistance (v 11)? No. Though Paul was in great "want/need" financially, he was not in want in terms of his contentment.

- **Why / why not?** Paul had learned a way to be "content" regardless of his circumstances or financial position. The word "content" (*autarkes*) was used of a country that had everything that it needed and where nothing had to be imported.

Such a country had all the resources and natural products needed to be self-sufficient. Nothing else was needed from the outside. Paul is finding his sense of joy and contentment somewhere other than in his situation or wealth.

4. When is Paul content (v 11-12)? When his circumstances are good or bad, up or down, positive or painful. Notice that Paul does not find contentment in prosperity when he is in that position, and he seeks it elsewhere in the times when he is in poverty, or hungry. No, he finds contentment in another source altogether, all the time, even when his circumstances are good.

5. Why is Paul content (v 13)? Here is the secret of contentment: "I can do all things through Him who strengthens me." First, Paul is content because he knows "Him"— the Lord Jesus. Paul's whole life is Christ (1 v 21), and he lacks nothing of Christ. He finds everything he needs in knowing his Savior and Lord. And it is through Christ that Paul possesses all the strength that he needs for his life. The word "strengthens" is the word that gives us "dynamite." The secret of contentment is to realize that you have everything you need for this life and for eternity in your relationship with Christ Jesus, and to rely upon and rest in him.

- **What do you think "all things" (or "all this") means (and does not mean) in this context?** It means that Christ will enable us to keep believing in him, and to do all that we need to in order to walk obediently as we follow him. It means that we live our lives knowing that the power of God is always greater than any difficulty we face. We can do all things that God calls us to do in his word. This verse has, however, been misunderstood, and misapplied, repeatedly over time. So it needs some qualification:

1. This does not mean God will empower me to sin. "All things/all this" would never include that which God hates or that which is opposed to his very nature.

2. This does not mean I can do supernatural physical feats, such as jump across the Atlantic Ocean or flap my arms and fly to the moon. It does not mean I can perform miracles. "All things" are the simple things of life that all believers are called to do.

3. This does not relieve me of my responsibility to commit myself to the means of grace—God's word, God's meal at the Lord's Supper, and so on. In other words, if I just sit back passively, I am not going to know this strength. It requires my active pursuit of the means of grace for me to experience this supernatural power in my life.

4. This does not remove my responsibility to confess my sin and to repent. If there is unconfessed, unrepentant sin in your life, it will pull the plug on your joy.

6. APPLY: What is the secret of contentment? It is to find all we need in knowing Christ—that he loves us, is in control of all things, and is working for our good; and that he gives us all we need to serve him. No outside aid is necessary. **Where else do we look, or point other Christians to, to find it? Why?** When we lack the contentment that Paul enjoyed and exemplified, it is not because we do not have what we need to enjoy it; it is because our eyes are on the wrong place. The world must seek contentment in places other than Christ, for it does not know Christ—and it is very easy for us unthinkingly to be swept along to those same places. Not only that, but we can without realizing it point other believers to the wrong places. For instance,

if someone has lost their job, in the way we speak with them we can easily suggest to them that contentment will be found in finding another, and perhaps a better, job. If someone is struggling with singleness and our response is to seek to introduce them to potential spouses, then we are suggesting to them that contentment will be found in being married.

7. APPLY: Is it harder to find contentment in Christ when times are hard, or when times are good? There is no right or wrong answer to this! The point is that we assume that contentment is easier when times are good—but when times are good, it is much easier to rely on worldly things for our sense of satisfaction. When Christ is all we have, it is often easier to realize that in truth he is all we need.

- **How does verse 13 teach us to speak to one another about contentment when:**
  - **things are going well?** Don't be fooled into thinking you do not need Christ. You are still called to obey him, and you still require his power to be at work in you to give you faith and to enable you to serve him.
  - **things are very hard?** Christ will not leave you unable… to believe in him; or to face what he is allowing you to go through; or to serve him in this trial. In what ways might he be teaching you to look to him and trust him?

8. How do these verses [v 14-23] reveal the partnership between Paul and the Philippian church?
- v 14: They "share with me in my affliction" or "troubles." "Share" here comes from the word *koinoueo*—it is repeated in v 15. What happens to Paul

matters to the church in Philippi.

- v 15-18: They have given financially, on several occasions, to support Paul in his ministry, and now in his imprisonment.
- v 21-22: Those with Paul greet all those in Philippi—there is a sense of kinship between them, even though almost none of them have met each other.

9. How does Paul describe the Philippians' financial giving in verse 18?
"A fragrant aroma, an acceptable sacrifice, well-pleasing to God." You may need to explain to your group that Paul is using the imagery of an Old Testament sacrifice being offered by the priest on the altar. In this act, incense was poured onto the sacrifice, releasing a fragrant aroma that ascended upward to heaven. The sweet-smelling fragrance pictured the pleasure that such a sacrifice brought to God. In like manner, the giving of the Philippian Christians is an expression of their worship of God that is well-pleasing to him.

- **What does he promise the Philippians about their finances in verse 19?** That God would "supply all your needs according to His riches in glory in Christ Jesus." Not only would the Philippians receive spiritual blessings in heaven for their giving; but God would also supply their physical needs in this life. **Why is it important that he says "needs" and not "wants" or "wishes"?** Because it is not a blank check for the Philippians to fill in. God knows what we need, and will ensure that we have it. But that may be different from what we want or wish for— or even what we think we need.

EXPLORE MORE
Read 2 Corinthians 8 v 1-5, 9-15; 9 v 6-11. Why did the Macedonian church give so sacrificially and joyfully (8 v 1-5, 9)?

- Because of God's grace, or kindness (v 1): giving is a privilege given by God.
- Because of their "abundance of joy" (v 2). If we have joy that is rooted in our relationship with Jesus Christ, then we will love to support his people financially, rather than clinging on to our wealth.
- Because they "first gave themselves to the Lord and to us" (v 5). When we are devoted to the Lord and his people, it will be natural to use whatever means we have to further his cause and support his people.
- Because (by implication) this church knew Christ's grace. They understood that he had given up far more than they had ever had, in order to stoop far lower than they ever would, so that they might enjoy treasure in heaven eternally. If we know what Christ did for us, then we will act in like manner toward others, giving up what we have in order to give to them.

What instructions for giving does Paul give in 8 v 10-15?

- v 10-11: Make sure you actually give, rather than merely intending to.
- v 12: God's opinion of the amount you give is based on the amount that you have. If you are poor, you do not need to compare your gift unfavorably with that of someone who is wealthy.
- v 13-15: The point of Christian financial giving is that every believer would enjoy some level of equality. Our giving is not to leave us needing support ourselves, or to mean that another believer has more than they need and never need work again.

What do his readers need to believe (9 v 6-11)? That those who give generously and sacrificially will find God ensuring they have what they themselves need. He will ensure that we are able to continue to give generously!

How does Paul's teaching here fit with,

and add to, his words to the Philippians about their giving? Many of the themes are similar. Giving is a privilege, a grace from God. We give generously and sacrificially because it pleases God. We are able to give because our joy is not based on what we own, but on whose we are. God is able to give us what we need as we give generously to those in need.

10. How are verses 20 and 23 fitting "Amens" with which to end this letter?
- v 20: Because God has so faithfully supplied Paul's needs, and because he promises to provide for the Philippians, the apostle has great reason to offer praise to him. But not only that—he is the God who finishes what he has started in his people, who sent his Son to die for us and then raised him and exalted him, who works in his people to sanctify them, and who gives us all joy and all we need in Christ. He is infinitely and eternally worthy of glory and praise!
- v 23: "Grace" (*karis*) is unmerited, undeserved favor in the lives of God's people. It is the wellspring and the heartbeat of the Christian life. The believers in Philippi had already received saving grace at the time of their regeneration. Paul nevertheless desires that they know more of this sanctifying grace in their Christian walk, which will enable them to live in a manner that glorifies God, and to do so with joy. The Christian life is all of grace.

11. APPLY: Paul says there is great joy in giving generously and sacrificially. How does this compare with the view of the society in which you live? Western societies tend to encourage us to treat our money as our own, to be spent on whatever we like. Often consumption is deliberately designed to be conspicuous—to make a statement to others. Giving tends to be out of what is left over once we have spent what we wish to, rather than taken from what we would otherwise spend on ourselves. And we are encouraged to make sure our futures are financially secure— which is wise to an extent, but not if it prevents us from trusting in God to provide what we need tomorrow, so that we are free to give today.
- **Which view do you tend to follow? How can you encourage each other as a church to listen to God's word in this area?** Discuss: how you talk about money; whether you prompt others to envy because of what you have, or spend; to what extent you are truly more like the Macedonian or Philippian churches than the culture around you.

12. APPLY: Think back over the whole letter. What reasons has Paul given you for shining with joy in your life? Which have most struck you and changed you, and why? Encourage your group each to write down a couple of particularly striking truths from the letter that they wish to remember and apply to their affections or their lives; and then share them together. It should provide a very encouraging end to your studies in the book of Philippians, and be a great spur to praise God as you close this session.

Good Book Guides
The full range

Galatians: 7 Studies
Timothy Keller
ISBN: 9781908762559

Ephesians: 10 Studies
Thabiti Anyabwile
ISBN: 9781907377099

Ephesians: 8 Studies
Richard Coekin
ISBN: 9781910307694

Philippians: 7 Studies
Steven J. Lawson
ISBN: 9781784981181

Colossians: 6 Studies
Mark Meynell
ISBN: 9781906334246

1 Thessalonians:
7 Studies
Mark Wallace
ISBN: 9781904889533

2 Timothy: 7 Studies
Mark Mulryne
ISBN: 9781905564569

Titus: 5 Studies
Tim Chester
ISBN: 9781909919631

Hebrews: 8 Studies
Justin Buzzard
ISBN: 9781906334420

James: 6 Studies
Sam Allberry
ISBN: 9781910307816

1 Peter: 5 Studies
Tim Chester
ISBN: 9781907377853

1 Peter: 6 Studies
Juan R. Sanchez
ISBN: 9781784980177

1 John: 7 Studies
Nathan Buttery
ISBN: 9781904889953

Revelation 2–3: 7 Studies
Jonathan Lamb
ISBN: 9781905564682

TOPICAL

Man of God: 10 Studies
Anthony Bewes & Sam Allberry
ISBN: 9781904889977

Biblical Womanhood:
10 Studies
Sarah Collins
ISBN: 9781907377532

The Apostles' Creed:
10 Studies
Tim Chester
ISBN: 9781905564415

Promises Kept Bible Overview: 9 Studies
Carl Laferton
ISBN: 9781908317933

Contentment: 6 Studies
Anne Woodcock
ISBN: 9781905564668

These truths alone: the Reformation Solas
6 Studies
Jason Helopoulos
ISBN: 9781784981501

Women of Faith:
8 Studies
Mary Davis
ISBN: 9781904889526

Meeting Jesus: 8 Studies
Jenna Kavonic
ISBN: 9781905564460

Heaven: 6 Studies
Andy Telfer
ISBN: 9781909919457

Making Work Work:
8 Studies
Marcus Nodder
ISBN: 9781908762894

The Holy Spirit: 8 Studies
Pete & Anne Woodcock
ISBN: 9781905564217

Experiencing God:
6 Studies
Tim Chester
ISBN: 9781906334437

Real Prayer: 7 Studies
Anne Woodcock
ISBN: 9781910307595

Dig Deeper into Philippians

PHILIPPIANS FOR YOU

Dr Lawson brings his trademark insights and passion to the letter to the Philippians. Written for Christians of every age and stage, whether new believers or pastors and teachers, each title in the series takes a detailed look at a part of the Bible in an expository, readable, relevant way.

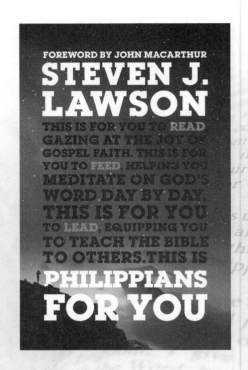

Philippians For You is for you:

- *to read*, mapping out the themes, promises and challenges of the epistle
- *to feed,* using it as a daily devotional, complete with helpful reflection questions
- *to lead,* equipping small-group leaders and Bible teachers and preachers to explain, illustrate and apply this wonderful book of the Bible.

Find out more at:
www.thegoodbook.com/for-you

with Steven Lawson

EXPLORE DAILY DEVOTIONAL

These devotionals help you open up the Scriptures and will encourage and equip you in your walk with God. Available as a book or as an app, *Explore* features Dr Lawson's notes on Philippians, alongside contributions from trusted Bible teachers including Albert Mohler, Mark Dever, Tim Keller, Sam Allberry, and Ray Ortlund.

Find out more at:
www.thegoodbook.com/explore

HARDBACK DEVOTIONALS
FOR DAILY BIBLE READING

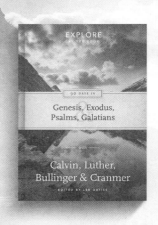

90 days with the Reformers in Genesis, Exodus, Psalms, and Galatians

Calvin, Luther, Bullinger & Cranmer

Open up the Bible with 90 devotions by famous Reformers including Luther and Calvin.
Edited by Dr Lee Gatiss.

Hardback | 288pp
ISBN: 9781784980863

90 Days in Ruth, Jeremiah, and 1 Corinthians

Mark Dever & Mike McKinley

Ninety days of open-Bible devotionals with Mark Dever and Mike McKinley. Includes space for journaling.

Hardback | 288pp
ISBN: 9781784981235

EXPLORE DEVOTIONALS
BY TIMOTHY KELLER

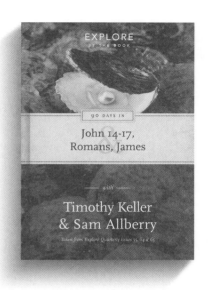

90 days in John 14–17, Romans, and James
Timothy Keller & Sam Allberry

Open up the Bible with 90 devotions by Timothy Keller and Sam Allberry. Includes space for journaling.

Hardback | 288pp
ISBN: 9781784981228

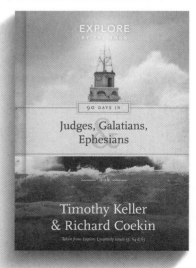

90 Days in Judges, Galatians, and Ephesians
Timothy Keller & Richard Coekin

Ninety days of open-Bible devotionals with Timothy Keller and Richard Coekin. Includes space for journaling.

Hardback | 288pp
ISBN: 9781784981631

thegoodbook
COMPANY

BIBLICAL | RELEVANT | ACCESSIBLE

At The Good Book Company, we are dedicated to helping Christians and local churches grow. We believe that God's growth process always starts with hearing clearly what he has said to us through his timeless word—the Bible.

Ever since we opened our doors in 1991, we have been striving to produce resources that honor God in the way the Bible is used. We have grown to become an international provider of user-friendly resources to the Christian community, with believers of all backgrounds and denominations using our Bible studies, books, evangelistic resources, DVD-based courses, and training events.

We want to equip ordinary Christians to live for Christ day by day, and churches to grow in their knowledge of God, their love for one another, and the effectiveness of their outreach.

Call us for a discussion of your needs or visit one of our local websites for more information on the resources and services we provide.

Your friends at The Good Book Company

NORTH AMERICA		thegoodbook.com		866 244 2165
UK & EUROPE		thegoodbook.co.uk		0333 123 0880
AUSTRALIA		thegoodbook.com.au		(02) 9564 3555
NEW ZEALAND		thegoodbook.co.nz		

 WWW.CHRISTIANITYEXPLORED.ORG
Our partner site is a great place for those exploring the Christian faith, with a clear explanation of the good news, powerful testimonies and answers to difficult questions.